When Anders Was Three

City Family Farm Family
Book 2

By Roslyn Ross

These stories take place in the year 2015.

These stories are mostly true. Some changes were made to make them more educational and to make them more entertaining.

1. Magic Sticks

There was a three-year-old boy named Anders. He had idealistic parents who wanted to do the ideal thing no matter what anyone else did. Last year, Tom and Roslyn (Anders called them Papa and Mama) came to think the ideal education for their son required living in two different places: on a farm and in a city.

So, Papa and Mama decided to do an experiment. They decided to live with Anders for half of the year on a farm in rural Nicaragua and the other half in a gigantic city called Los Angeles.

Right now, the family of three were living at the farm in Nicaragua. It wasn't much of a farm yet though.

There was no barn or farmhouse. There were just a few rough cement rooms where the family slept and a three-sided wooden building with a camping stove and a picnic table where they cooked and ate. The only bathroom was a rough cement building with a bucket toilet.

The only animals at the farm right now were a small mutt named Brava, a few chickens, and a cow that didn't make milk.

The only food-producing plants were some pepper bushes that grew wild in various places on the property, a few old mango trees, and one old *jocote* tree. (*Jocotes* are similar to cherries.) That was it.

Two workers lived at the farm with Papa, Mama, and Anders—Nate and James. Nate worked as the farm manager. He was Mama's cousin from Montana in the United States. He was six feet and three inches tall, good looking, always happy, and tough. Many local women wanted to date him.

Nate had been living at the farm since August 2013. This year a man, named James, joined him. James was a retired English professor from Washington in the United States. He was a stylish dresser with a dry sense of humor. He wanted to learn Spanish, so he made a trade with Papa and Mama: he would cook six days a week for Papa, Mama, Anders, Nate, and himself, and in exchange he would get room and board at the farm, a small salary, and plenty of free time to practice Spanish with the neighbors.

Papa, Mama, and Anders planned for their land to be a farm one day, and they already referred to it as a farm, but at this point, it was just land, land that had been used as cow pasture for a few decades. Before that it had been jungle. Papa, Mama, and Anders had a lot of work to do to turn the land into a farm.

The first thing they had to do was get water. There was no river or waterfall on the property, just a little creek that was dry for half of the year.

"We are going to have to dig a well," Papa told Mama and Anders.

"What's a well?" Anders asked

"It's a big hole in the ground," Papa said. "If you dig down far enough in the right spot, there is water down there."

"How big will the hole be?" Anders asked excitedly.

"Really big," Papa said.

"This big?" Anders asked, opening his arms as wide as he could.

a camping stove

"Bigger!" Papa said. Papa opened his arms as wide as *he* could, which was a lot wider. "It will even be bigger than this!"

"Wow," Anders said.

"And so deep that the hole will go way over your head. It might be so deep that you won't even be able to see the bottom," Papa said.

"Wow," Anders said again. "I love wells!"

That day Max, the contractor who had built the few rough buildings on the farm, came to the farm with a man named Juan. Juan was of medium height and medium build, which meant he was about half a foot shorter than Papa. (Papa was six feet one inches tall.) Juan wore jeans and a T-shirt. He carried a Y-shaped stick that was about two feet long. After greeting the family, he went straight to work, walking around the property while concentrating intently on the Y-shaped stick. The long part of the stick he held out in front of him toward the ground.

Juan was called a water witch. A water witch is a person who uses a stick to determine where people should dig their wells.

"I can't believe you hired a water witch," Mama said, shaking her head at the spectacle. Papa and Mama did not believe there was any such thing as a magical stick that would tell someone where to dig a well.

"Even if I don't believe in magical water-finding sticks, Max does," Papa explained. "Max wouldn't start this project without the town water witch signing off on it."

"That's so interesting," Mama said. "How much did the witch cost?"

"A thousand *córdobas*," Papa said. "About forty dollars."

"By local standards that is a lot of money. Do you think it's a scam?" Mama asked.

"What's a scam?" Anders asked.

"See that Y-shaped stick Juan is holding out?" Papa asked. "Do you think that that stick has a mind of its own and will bend closer to the ground where we should dig the well? Do you think sticks can move on their own or do you think people move them?"

"People move them," Anders said. "Or the wind."

"That's what I think too, Anders," Papa said. "But that is not what Max thinks. Max thinks that Juan has a special stick that bends on its own."

"That's silly," Anders said.

"Yes," Papa agreed. "The question is: What does Juan think? Does Juan genuinely believe he has a magical stick, or is he tricking Max to get some money?"

"He's tricking Max," Anders said.

"That's what a scam is. When you trick people," Papa explained.

"Ooooh," Anders said, nodding.

"I also think Juan is tricking Max," Mama added. "But it's possible that Juan doesn't know it. Maybe he tricked himself first. Maybe he genuinely believes he has a magical stick. That's a good question for you, Anders. If Juan genuinely believes his stick is magical—does that mean it is?"

Anders thought about this for a little bit.

"No," he decided.

"That's right," Mama said. "Just because Juan believes something, does not mean it is true. We must use our own brains to examine the evidence and decide."

"And we also want to keep an open mind," Papa added. "Maybe we are wrong. Maybe there are magic sticks. I have never seen one, but maybe they exist, and I just haven't seen them. It's important to stay humble, so that our brains stay open and willing to accept new information."

Papa, Mama, and Anders watched Juan for a few minutes. Juan was walking in the swampy area behind the rancho. He had rubber boots on, but he walked carefully, staying on top of dirt mounds and plants and out of the mud.

Then he took a wrong step.

Juan put his foot on what looked like a tuft of wild grass, but it turned out to be grass growing thickly in a large, deep mud puddle. Juan's foot immediately sank down, all the way to the bottom of the puddle. The puddle was deeper than Juan's boot. His boot filled with muddy water

"Ugh!" Juan said, wobbling back and forth before catching his balance. He pulled his boot out of the hole and turned it over to pour out the muddy water. When he put it back on, every time he took a step, it went *squish*.

"I think he found some water," Anders said. Papa and Mama laughed.

"What I don't understand is why he didn't come in costume," Mama said. "If I'm going to pay someone to pretend to be a witch, the least they could do is look the part."

Papa laughed.

Then he said, "That's how we know he is tricking himself too and not just tricking Max. If he made a big show of it by wearing a costume and doing dramatic things, we would know that he knows his stick isn't really magical."

"What if both Max and Juan know the stick is not magical, and they are tricking us for an extra forty dollars?" Mama asked.

"That's possible," Papa said. "But if that's the case, then it's just part of the cost of digging the well. But I don't think so. Max is always talking about spirits and ghosts and stuff. I think he genuinely believes Juan has a magic stick."

The family watched Juan for a while longer.

Squish, squish went Juan's boots.

"I wish you would have gone with the professional well-digging company from the city," Mama said.

Papa nodded. He knew that's what Mama would have preferred, but he really wanted a hand-dug well rather than a machine-drilled one. He wanted things on the farm to be done the old-fashioned way.

"The hand-dug well will cost a lot less—if it works," Papa said.

Mama bit her tongue. She had said her piece before, and she had decided to let Papa make what she believed was a mistake.

"I value my freedom to make mistakes," Mama had explained to Anders. "And, just as much, I respect your father's right to make mistakes. And yours. Mistakes are how we learn. But sometimes mistakes are costly."

"Maybe the well will work," Anders had said hopefully. "Maybe it won't be a mistake."

After an hour or so, Juan, the water witch, announced that the well should be dug in the swampy area where he had gotten stuck in the mud. He pronounced that if they dug in that spot, they would hit water.

Papa thought that sounded logical—the area clearly had water since it was swampy. So, Papa gave Max permission to start the project.

2. Bring Your Kids to Life

At 6:30 the next morning, Max's old, beat-up pickup truck bumped up the driveway and groaned to a stop. In the bed of the truck were pickaxes, shovels, buckets, ropes, and five men.

The men hopped out of the truck, carried their digging supplies to the well site, and got right to work.

Max pounded a wooden stake into the spot that Juan had chosen for the well. Max then tied a rope to the stake. He measured four feet and then moved the rope in a circle around the stake, making a circle with a four-foot radius. (The radius is the distance from the center point to the edge of a circle. In this case the stake was where the center of the well would be.) Each worker picked a place along the circumference of the circle and began digging.

Anders thought what the workers were doing looked like great fun, so he joined them. He had a shovel just his size and was an expert digger. The dirt where the well was being dug was thick, wet, and claylike, so it was much more difficult to dig up than regular, dry dirt.

The workers loved that Anders wanted to help, so they made piles of loose clay for him to move from inside the circle to outside. Anders was happy to be included, and he was genuinely useful.

Anders loved seeing the piles of dirt outside the circle grow larger and larger. He helped with the well on and off for the rest of the morning. Watching Anders dig with the men warmed Mama's heart.

"Instead of bring-your-kids-to-work day, once a year," she mused, "how about bring-your-kids-to-*life*, every day? Children are so happy to be included in real work."

The sun rose and it became very hot. By 11:00am it was time to break for lunch. The workers ate and then fell asleep.

After an hour, Max woke them, and they went back to digging. They dug until 3:30 in the afternoon, when they were done for the day. Then Max and the workers piled into Max's truck and went home.

This was the best part of the day. Anders had delighted in working with the men, but now, with no workers there, he could have the whole digging area to himself.

Anders gathered his toy construction trucks and placed them in various piles of dirt near the not-very-deep-yet well. There he happily played until it was dark.

The workers returned the next day and, again, dug all day. Again, Anders helped as much as he chose to.

The digging was arduous, but every day, there was progress—the well got a little deeper. More importantly to Anders, the piles of dirt around the well site grew larger. And every day, Anders looked forward to when the workers went home, and he could have the piles of dirt all to himself. He was a happy boy.

A month passed in this way. The claylike mud went on and on. Then the workers hit rock. Breaking through rock with crow bars was even slower work than digging through clay, but Anders loved that too. Rock dust and broken rock chunks were wonderful additions to Anders's dirt piles.

Max hoped there would be water below the rock, but there wasn't. There was just more sticky, clay mud.

One day the workers did not want Anders to help anymore.

Anders ran to Mama and reported, "Mama! They won't let me help!"

He was crushed. His face streamed with tears.

Mama lifted Anders into her arms and hugged him. When he was done crying, she walked with him to the well site to see what the problem was.

"It's too deep now," Max explained in Spanish. "It's dangerous."

Mama looked at the impressive hole. The men were using a ladder to climb in and out of it now. Only two or three men could dig at a time. They filled buckets for the other men to hoist out of the hole with ropes, empty, and lower back down to the digging men.

"They are worried about you falling in," Mama explained to Anders. "It's dangerous."

"I won't fall in," Anders said.

Anders was annoyed. And rightly so. Anders was three years old, but he had never fallen *in his life*—not even when he was learning to walk. He had never hit his head; he had never had a scraped knee. He was like a monkey and climbed all over the place, but he was careful. Mama appreciated that about him.

"You are a safe and responsible boy," Mama agreed. "That is why I usually let you be in charge of your safety. I say, 'Well, it won't kill you, but it could hurt,' and then I let you decide. But the well is getting deep enough that if you fell in accidentally, it *could* kill you. If there is a reasonable chance something can kill you, it's better safe than... dead."

"Better safe than dead!" Anders repeated with deep understanding. "Okay, Mama. I don't want to be dead."

The workers at the top of the well hole carted wheelbarrows of dirt to a nearby tree. They made those piles even bigger than the piles that had been near the well. They told Anders he could play in those piles of dirt. Anders was elated. Now he had three huge piles of dirt, and he didn't have to wait for the workers to go home to have them all to himself.

"Thank you!" Anders yelled to them in Spanish.

Over the next few weeks Anders spent so much time in his dirt piles that wherever he went, he left a trail of dirt behind him. Whenever he sat down anywhere, he left an unmistakable Anders-print. One time he was so dirty Mama pretended she couldn't even see him.

"Why is this pile of dirt talking to me?" Mama asked.

"I'm not a pile of dirt! I'm your son!" Anders exclaimed.

Mama looked confusedly at Anders. "No, my son is a boy," she said. "You are a boy-sized pile of dirt! I must go look for my son now. Let me know if you see him."

3. No Thank You Blah

Life was tough at the farm during this time. It was ninety degrees and humid most days. There was only one medium-sized room with an air conditioning unit. That was the only air conditioning at the farm, so that was the room the family stayed in. The only furniture in the room was two beds, one desk, and one chair. There were no bedside tables, dressers, closets, or shelves, so all the family's things were organized in suitcases and plastic tubs on the floor. The room had a single lightbulb that hung from the ceiling. It provided so little light that Mama had to wear her headlamp when she was organizing the suitcases.

Then there was the rancho, the rough, wooden building with only three sides that had a kitchen and dining area. The kitchen area had a wooden counter, a camping stove, a refrigerator that leaked, and a sink. The dining area, right next to the kitchen area, had a picnic table where the family ate. This meant they were always exposed to the elements while they were eating. It also meant that no meal was eaten without constantly shooing flies and wasps away and swatting a few mosquitos.

The small, cement bathroom had two enclosed stalls. One stall had a bucket toilet. The other had a shower. Both stalls had openings near the ceiling for windows, but there was no glass in the window spaces yet. Though the stalls had doors, the building did not. This meant there was rarely a trip to the bathroom that did not involve some kind of insect encounter.

Though there was a shower, there was no usable water at the farm right. Usable water was delivered each week in five-gallon jugs by a water-delivery truck. This meant water was quite expensive. Even though everyone sweated every day in the intense heat, bathing was a luxury no one indulged in more than once a week. Except Anders. He took a bath in a five-gallon bucket every night. He was simply too dirty at the end of each day not to.

The farm had no internet, no television, and no radio. Before leaving Los Angeles, Mama had downloaded some documentaries to her laptop. Anders enjoyed watching them during the hottest part of the day, when Mama wanted him to stay inside.

Anders's favorite documentaries were about bees, penguins, cows, dolphins, and babies. Even though Anders enjoyed watching documentaries, he preferred playing outside, especially when kids from neighboring farms came over.

Mama preferred being inside. She stayed in the air-conditioned bedroom most of the day writing. She also studied philosophy and objective beauty in architectural design.

Papa, like Anders, preferred being outside. He walked the property endlessly, deciding where swales, pastures, forests, and gardens should go. He also did plenty of reading about farming because he knew little about it. He wanted to learn how to care for plants and animals, how to improve the soil, and how to create a microclimate that would make the property cooler and wetter.

One morning Papa said, "I want a break from the farm. Do you guys want to go on an adventure?"

"Yes!" said Mama.

"Yes!" said Anders.

They drove to a small fishing village about forty minutes away called Morrito. Morrito was on Lake Nicaragua, a large lake in the middle of the country.

Papa drove down a pothole-pocked street that followed the shoreline. Between the street and the water was lush, green land with many large rocks. Chickens scratched and pecked there for bugs. Closer to the shore, there were many different types of birds. It was hard to tell where the shore ended and the lake began because of all the reeds and other plants in the shallow water.

The only thing that marred the natural beauty of the area was the trash that seemed to be everywhere.

Papa parked the car near a long cement dock in the middle of town. He called out to a man in a fishing boat to ask about restaurants nearby. The fisherman said there was only one and pointed it out to Papa. It was a patio outside someone's home with a rough wooden sign that said, "Restaurant."

Papa, Mama, and Anders walked down the street to the restaurant. They passed houses where people sat outside in inactivity. When the family arrived at the restaurant, a man invited them to sit down at a small table.

He brought over a chalkboard on which the menu was written in English. It read: breakfast three dollars, lunch four dollars, and dinner five dollars. Mama ordered three lunches.

Even though Papa, Mama, and Anders were the only customers in the restaurant, it took an hour and a half for their food to arrive. When it did, Mama was excited to see a whole, cooked fish on each person's plate. The waiter, most likely the owner of the home, said the fish had been caught fresh that morning. It was served on a bed of rice with tomato sauce and plantains. (Plantains are similar to bananas.) Mama asked the man if the people in Morrito ate a lot of fish. He said they had fish for lunch and dinner every day.

"Did you guys see the waiter's teeth?" Mama asked. "They are so straight and white and beautiful! Everyone I have seen so far in this town has perfect teeth. I wonder if it's because of all the fish they eat."

Papa and Anders weren't listening. They were digging into their fish and rice.

"Ooooooh this is tasty!" said Papa.

"Suuuuuper tasty," Anders said.

"I don't know," Mama said, tasting hers. "The tomato sauce tastes strange. Too sweet. It has a chemical aftertaste."

Because Mama had been raised on farm food and had been exposed to little processed food in her life, she didn't like the way processed food tasted. She could reliably tell if something she was eating had artificial flavors or flavor enhancers.

Five minutes after they started eating, Anders's cheeks turned bright red, something that only happened when he ate processed food. Mama asked the restaurant owner about the ingredients in the tomato sauce. He brought out a jar of sauce and a flavor packet and explained to Mama how the sauce was made. Mama read the ingredients on the jar and the flavor packet.

Papa, on the other hand, was raised on processed food. Though he rarely ate it now that he knew better, he still liked how chemical flavor enhancers tasted.

"Anders," Mama said, "I'm so sorry. I was not expecting this, but we just ate MSG, artificial flavors, and high-fructose corn syrup."

"That explains why it was so tasty!" Papa joked.

"Are you feeling okay?" Mama asked Anders, who always got sick when he ate processed food.

"I feel fine," Anders said, but right after they left the restaurant, Anders vomited on the sidewalk.

"I guess that was a dumb question," Mama said. "You always feel fine. You just vomit."

Papa, Mama, and Anders headed back to toward the restaurant to ask for supplies to clean up the vomit, but as soon as they had walked a few steps away from the vomit, thin, stray dogs appeared and began licking it up.

"That is so gross, I might vomit," Mama said.

"At least we don't have to worry about cleaning it up," Papa offered.

They walked to the other side of the street to give the dogs plenty of space.

"Anders, your body is so awesome," Papa said admiringly. "You try to feed your body chemicals, and your body says, 'No thank you, blah!'"

Anders laughed. "No thank you! Blah!" he repeated over and over for the rest of the day.

4. Strange Smoke in San Carlos

Now Papa was back in Los Angeles. He could only be gone from his company for a few weeks at a time. Mama and Anders stayed at the farm, so they could oversee the well-digging project. They also wanted to continue getting to know Nicaragua.

Mama and Anders missed Papa terribly and called him every day. For every phone call they had to get in the truck and drive a mile down the road to the nearest place where they could find a cell signal.

"How is life at the farm?" Papa asked one day on the phone.

"Nothing has changed," Mama said. "The guys are still working on the well every day."

"How deep is it now?" Papa asked.

"So deep that they can't use a ladder anymore. Now they have a rope that they use to climb in and out of it," Mama said.

"Wow," Papa said. "Climbing up ropes is so hard! Are you guys planning any new adventures?"

"Yes," Mama said. "Tomorrow we are headed to San Carlos. It is the closest city to the south of us. Max says it is a small city on the water and has good fish."

"Is it safe?" Papa asked.

"Max says it is. He says it has a nice hotel with air conditioning, Wi-Fi, and hot water."

"Oooh," Papa said. "I bet you are looking forward to that."

"I am!" Mama said. "And James is going to come with us. I feel safer traveling with a man."

"That sounds great," Papa said. "I am glad James is going with you. Criminals are always looking for the easiest target. A mom and a child are definitely an easier target than a mom and a child who have a man with them."

"The only thing I don't like is that I can't find any information on the hotel. There isn't a single hotel in San Carlos that has a website, so we will be driving there without knowing where we are going to sleep."

"If it doesn't feel safe, turn around and drive back to the farm," Papa said.

"That's the plan," Mama said. "Max told us that the nice hotel is called the Coconuts, and its right on the main square, so hopefully we won't have any issues finding it."

"Well, I wish you a fun adventure full of incredible luxuries like air conditioning, Wi-Fi, and hot water," Papa said.

"Fingers crossed," Mama said. "So many times hotels here say they have those things and then the hot water is 'broken' or the Wi-Fi is 'down.'"

The next day, after two quick hours of driving, Mama, Anders, and James arrived in San Carlos. They drove around the town square looking for the Coconuts Hotel. They did not find it. They went into two different stores and asked for directions to the Coconuts Hotel, but no one had heard of it.

Just then they saw huge clouds of smoke billowing from the downtown area. Mama heard a sound that sounded like a foghorn.

"Maybe that's what their fire warnings sound like," Mama said, quickly ushering everyone in the truck to drive them a safe distance away.

Mama expected to hear sounds of distress and see other cars driving away—after all, there was a lot of smoke! But not only did Mama not see or hear any sounds of fire, other cars proceeded right into town, right into the smoke, as if their drivers weren't concerned at all. And it wasn't just nonchalant drivers—pedestrians lounged outside of buildings, inhaling the smoke. They walked down the sidewalk toward the smoke like it was no big deal.

Mama drove to the outskirts of town where the air was clear and parked the truck outside a small hostel. She inquired one last time about the Coconuts Hotel. The hostel workers had not heard of it either.

Changing tactics, Mama asked, "What would you say is the nicest hotel in town?"

"*Esquina del Lago*," said the hostel manager. In English the name meant *Corner of the Lake*. "It's not quite in town though, it's on an island in the lake. You must take a boat to get there."

"That sounds amazing!" Mama said. "You don't by any chance have their phone number, do you?"

The hostel manager did have the hotel's phone number and gave it to Mama. Mama spoke with a hotel staff member on the phone. The hotel had internet, but it did not have hot water or air conditioning. Mama thought about heading back to the farm, but then the man on the phone told her that the hotel offered cruises up the river.

"That sounds like it could be an interesting adventure," Mama thought. She arranged to meet the hotel's boat at the pier in one hour.

Before she left the hostel, Mama inquired about the strange smoke.

"Are they having some kind of bonfire in town or something?" Mama asked.

The owner of the hostel said there was no fire: they were fumigating for mosquitos.

"And everyone just stands there and breathes in the pesticides?" Mama asked.

"Yeah," the hostel manager said, shrugging.

Mama was aghast. One of the reasons Papa and she wanted to live on a farm was to give their bodies a break from the toxic air in Los Angeles. She didn't want to breathe toxic air in Nicaragua too!

Mama returned to the truck and told Anders and James what she had learned about the "smoke." She drove five minutes further down the highway away from the town, so they wouldn't be exposed to the pesticide. Then she parked the truck on the side of the road.

"We can wait here until the pesticide clears," Mama said.

Anders took his seatbelt off and climbed onto Mama's lap for a cuddle.

"Soooo, do you want to hear about the hotel I found?" Mama asked, taking Anders's hand.

"Yes!" Anders said.

"What hotel did you find?" James asked.

"A hotel that is on an island that we have to take a boat to get to," Mama said.

James was excited for the adventure. Anders's mouth hung open in awe.

"I have always wanted to go on a boat!" Anders said excitedly.

Mama squeezed him tight. Then, feeling excited and silly, she took Anders's hand and started hitting his leg with it.

"Anders," she said, "why are you hitting yourself?"

Anders looked at his hand—being controlled by Mama—hitting his leg. Then he looked at Mama. She was being silly.

"Seriously, Anders," Mama said, making his hand swat his belly. "Why are you hitting yourself? It's concerning. I'm worried about you."

Anders giggled. He tensed the muscles in his arm, so Mama couldn't make him hit himself. Then Mama took his foot and made him start kicking himself.

"And now you're kicking yourself! What's wrong, Anders? Is there something you need to talk about?" Mama asked, smiling.

Anders laughed and laughed.

5. Not Wanting to Clean Up

Mama parked the truck in the pier parking lot. A man wearing a polo shirt that said *Hotel Esquina del Lago* was waiting there.

The man introduced himself in as Pierre. He took Mama's suitcase and walked with her, James, and Anders down the pier to where the hotel's boat was waiting. The boat was small and silver with an outboard motor, a motor that attached to the back of the boat and dipped into the water. *Esquina del Lago* was painted on the side of the boat.

stilt

The ride to the hotel took ten minutes. Anders sat on Mama's lap and enjoyed every minute of it. He loved the feel of the wind on his face. He turned his head in every direction to see the sights. He watched the view of the town get smaller and smaller as they traveled farther away. The boat captain pointed out a dozen different kinds of birds: stilts, oyster catchers, storks, pelicans, herons, and even a toucan.

"These birds are so beautiful!" said Anders.

Shortly they arrived at the hotel. It was on a tiny island, an island so small that the hotel took up the entire thing. Pierre secured the boat to the dock, and everyone disembarked.

Hotel Esquina del Lago was a fishing lodge owned by a Frenchman named Philippe. Philippe had lived in Nicaragua for thirty years. His son was named Pierre. Pierre was the man who had navigated the motorboat. He was in his twenties. He lived on the island and helped run the hotel.

Esquina del Lago mainly catered to groups of men who came for sport-fishing trips. The rooms

oyster catcher

were sparse and uncomfortable. The windows did not have glass, just screens, and the beds had netting over them to protect sleeping guests from biting insects. There was no internet or cell service in the rooms, but there was an occasional cell signal and extremely slow internet in the dining area.

Dinner was genuinely tasty: fish, rice, a vegetable sauce, fried plantains (no flavor packets this time), and best of all, French bread made at the hotel and served fresh out of the oven with butter.

stork

After dinner Mama and Anders walked around the lodge, tried rocking in every hammock, enjoyed the view of the water, and spent a long time examining the various fish trophies that hung on the walls. There were snook, bass, *guapote*, and monster tarpon trophies. Philippe stopped by and told Anders fun stories about his fishing trips.

pelican

When Anders was done talking to Philippe, he and Mama found a checkerboard and began to play. But after a few minutes Anders became frustrated with the game. He took his arm and wiped the board. All the pieces were swept onto the floor.

"Oh dear," Mama said, "I think you are tired."

"Yes," Anders said. "I am too tired to pick up all the pieces."

Mama nodded. "That makes sense, we have had a busy day. Well, what should we do? We can't leave the pieces on the floor."

"You pick them up, Mama. I'm too tired," Anders said with gusto.

heron

"I don't think that would be right since you are the one who threw them on the floor," Mama said.

toucan

This was quite a dilemma. Mama did not want to make threats and get mad at Anders, but she thought he should pick up the pieces.

"How can I support him in doing this task he does not want to do?" she questioned herself. She knew that three-year-olds cooperate best when things are silly and fun, so she got out her phone and put on a timer.

"How about we make a bet?" Mama asked mischievously. "I bet... you cannot pick up all the pieces in less than ten seconds."

This did not sound like enough fun to Anders, so Mama tried again.

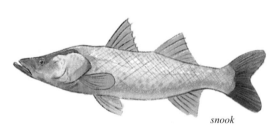

snook

"How about you start in that corner over there by the tarpon trophy, and you have to run over here to where the game pieces are, and you can only pick up the red pieces. And if you accidentally pick up a black piece you lose, but if you pick up all the red pieces in less than fifteen seconds, you win?"

Anders loved this idea. "Okay!" he said,

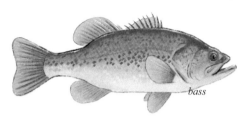

bass

running to the corner by the tarpon trophy.

"On your mark, get set, go!" Mama said.

Anders raced from the corner to the checkers pieces. He carefully picked up the red pieces while Mama counted the time. "One, two, three, four…."

Just as Mama was starting to say, "Fifteen," Anders picked up the last red checker. "Ahhh! You won! Oh my gosh I did not think you would make it!"

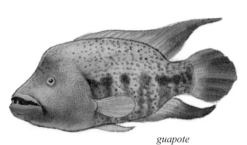

guapote

Mama exclaimed.

"I won!" Anders said. "Let's do it again!"

"Perfect," Mama said, "because the black pieces still need to be picked up! Okay, back to the tarpon trophy."

This time Anders did not make it. He picked up the last black piece just as Mama was saying "sixteen."

"You did so well," Mama said. "You are just too tired. Let's go to bed."

"I am going to fall asleep so fast," Anders said.

"I know you will," Mama said. "Probably before your head even hits your pillow."

monster tarpon

Anders fell asleep the moment he got into bed. He slept like a rock, as he usually did. Mama slept barely at all, as she had expected, considering the humidity and the bugs.

Whenever Mama had slept in beds with bug netting, she had still woken up with bug bites. This time was no exception. Anders awoke the next morning with many bug bites too.

"I don't want to stay a second night," Mama said. "How about you? Do you want to go back to the farm today or sleep here again?"

"The farm!" Anders said.

"I can't believe that as rough as our farm is right now, we would rather sleep there than at the nicest hotel in San Carlos," Mama said. "That must be a milestone or something. Hey—do you want to do a cruise down the river before we go home?"

"Yeah!" Anders said.

6. Real Jungle Cruise

Mama, James, and Anders boarded a small motorboat outfitted with both a shading canopy and an English-speaking guide. They were headed down the river. The cruise reminded Mama of the Jungle Cruise ride at Disneyland, but in this

caiman

version, the jungle was real.

Anders delighted in seeing caiman, otters, turtles, snakes, iguanas, exotic birds, white faced monkeys, and, in a tree overhanging the river, howler monkeys.

"Why aren't they howling?" Anders asked the guide.

iguana

"They are sleeping," the guide explained. "They sleep during the day."

Last year Mama had heard the howls of howling monkeys when she and Anders stayed at Selva Negra. Anders had been curious about them ever since.

"I really wanted to hear them howl," Anders said, disappointed but without whining. Anders never whined.

The guide stopped the boat.

"Hey monkeys!" he yelled at the monkeys in the tree above them. "Anders wants to hear you howl! Can you howl for

white faced monkey

him? He's a nice boy. Let's give him what he wants!"

The monkeys kept sleeping. The guide drove the boat to the shore which was covered in small pebbles. He reached down and grabbed a handful. Then he drove the boat back to where they had been, right below the monkeys, and began throwing small pebbles at them.

"Oh, that's okay, we can let them sleep," Mama said, trying to stop the guide.

He wouldn't hear of it. He just smiled at Mama and winked.

"Stop being lazy!" he yelled at the monkeys. One monkey woke from his slumber and looked down at the man hollering at him. The monkey made a small noise. The guide yelled and threw another pebble.

Soon other monkeys were waking up and moving about the tree. The guide kept yelling at them and throwing pebbles. Mama was a little frightened. There were many more monkeys than humans.

But there was nothing to be worried about. The guide knew howler monkeys. He knew how to rile them up just enough to make them howl.

And howl they did. After a few more pebbles and hollers, five or six monkeys awoke and started making shockingly loud, guttural, creepy-sounding howls[1] while swinging around on the branches of the trees over the river.

Anders was dumbfounded. He could not believe how loud the monkeys were. He put his hands over his ears.

"Thank you," he said to the guide, "but I don't want to hear them anymore. Can you make them stop?"

---

[1] I recommend doing an internet search for "howling monkeys howling" to get an idea of what they sound like.

The guide laughed and started the boat's motor.

"Bye guys!" Mama said, waving to the monkeys as they sped away. "Sorry for waking you up!"

7. Fairy Godmothers

Mama and Anders had been back at the farm for only two weeks since their adventure in San Carlos, but Mama was already wanting to escape from the farm again.

Mama loved the focus and productivity of life at the farm. With people to cook and clean, and with no internet, there was nothing to distract Mama from her work. She got so much done! But she had a long list of things she had read about in her architecture books that she wanted to look up on the internet. She was also aching for those little luxuries she had never noticed before living at the farm: hot water, good water pressure, bedside tables, bathrooms with four walls, flush toilets, and bug free dining.

"We didn't get a break from the bugs on our adventure to San Carlos the other week," Mama told Anders. "I have so many bug bites right now. I spend all day scratching. And you have so many bug bites, you look like you have a disease. I want to go to a hotel with no bugs for a few days. Do you want to come with me?"

"Yes!" Anders said excitedly. "Can the hotel have a swimming pool?"

"Of course," Mama said. "The hotel I am thinking of has a pool and their restaurant serves one of your favorite things—a cheese and charcuterie plate."

Charcuterie is sausages, ham, pâtés, and other cooked or processed meat foods. Cheese and charcuterie plates are usually served with bread, crackers, fruits, jams, honey, olives, pickles, mustards and other things that would taste good with the specific cheeses and meats on the plate. Anders liked to make his own little sandwiches and try all the different things that came on the plate.

"A cheese and charcuterie plate! Let's go there!" Anders said with enthusiasm.

"Do you want to go today?" Mama asked

"I will miss Yesnir too much. Can he come?" asked Anders.

"We can invite him," said Mama.

Anders's best friend in Nicaragua was Yesnir, a boy who lived on a farm across the highway. He was almost ten years old, helpful, kind, and tough. He brought his sister Jesslyn, who was four years old, to play with three-year-old Anders almost every day. The three of them had a riotous good time.

Mama told Yesnir that she and Anders would be going to the city of Managua for two nights, and he was welcome to come if he wanted to. Yesnir was excited. He had never been more than twenty miles from his family's farm. He had never been to a hotel or a restaurant or a shopping mall. He had never seen a city in real life. His mom said he could go.

"Yay!" said Anders.

"Go get your stuff," Mama said to Yesnir in Spanish. "We will leave in an hour."

An hour later Mama, Yesnir, and Anders piled into the truck and headed to Managua. It was a three-hour drive. Anders fell asleep right away. Yesnir looked out the window the entire drive.

When they got to the city, Mama drove to the Los Robles Hotel. Mama had compiled a list of hotels from a travel website. She was systematically staying at all the most beautiful hotels in Managua to study local architectural styles.

Los Robles was a lovely boutique hotel. A boutique hotel is a hotel with ten to a hundred rooms. Los Robles had twelve rooms.

Los Robles had a courtyard restaurant and a small pool. A trellis covered in flowers provided a beautiful roof for the chairs on one side of the pool. At first Mama thought she would build a similar trellis at the farm, but then she noted that the flowers fell on the pool chairs, making them sticky. The flowers also attracted bugs. Mama thought the farm had enough bugs already, so she decided not to build a trellis that might attract more.

After the Mama, Anders, and Yesnir settled into their rooms, Mama took the boys to a department store called Siman where she bought Yesnir some swimming trunks.

At the farm Yesnir had always swum in his boxers, but Mama did not think that was appropriate for a hotel. Siman also sold backpacks, pencils, paper, erasers, dictionaries, calculators, and other school supplies. Mama told Yesnir to grab what he needed for school, and she would buy those for him as well.

Yesnir's family was poor. Mama had grown up poor herself. When she was eleven years old her sixth-grade teacher, Katey O'Brien, had given Mama a job cleaning her classroom and grading papers for her after school for three dollars an hour.[2]

Mama worked for Mrs. O'Brien for four years. During that time Mrs. O'Brien, in addition to paying Mama for the hours she worked, had also given Mama gifts like taking her to restaurants, to see plays, and even on a few weekend trips that were like heaven to Mama when she was a child.

Mama called Katey O'Brien her Fairy Godmother for all the good she had brought into her life. Mama wanted to do for Yesnir what Mrs. O'Brien had done for her. She decided that when they got back to the farm, she would offer Yesnir paid work for a few hours a day if he wanted it.

Many people did not think children should be allowed to work. In fact, in the United States it was illegal for children to work for money. Mama thought this was one of the greatest tragedies to have ever

---

[2] I was paid four dollars an hour the second year I worked for her, and five dollars an hour for the two years after that. To make this amount of money as an eleven-year-old was amazing. For perspective, the minimum wage in California at the time was $5.05 an hour.

happened to children. First, because it removed them from the adult world and infantilized them. Second, because most children loved earning money. Third, because working was incredibly educational—in many ways, it was more educational than school; it was certainly more practical. And fourth, because being able to work and earn money from a young age was the most important activity Mama herself had had as a child. It taught her far more than school or any other activity she did. Moreover, having a job made Mama feel responsible, valued, and capable. Having her own money had given her freedom, choices, and pride.

Mama thought it was insane that children were expected to do schoolwork all day every day without any say in the matter and without getting paid, but it was not legal for them to do work that they chose to do and that paid them money. Not to mention that children were allowed to work in the entertainment industry. The whole thing made no sense to Mama.

For the entire history of humanity children had worked beside their parents—gathering food, hunting, farming, and operating stores.

"There were situations where children were exploited," Mama thought, "but the solution isn't to bar them from all paid work. That's throwing the baby out with the bathwater."

8. Using Taxis Safely

After their shopping trip, Mama, Anders, and Yesnir ate dinner at the hotel restaurant. Mama ordered fish for her entrée. Anders ordered a cheese and charcuterie plate for his. Yesnir didn't want any of the entrees. He wanted a regular dinner: rice, beans, tortillas, sour cream, some meat or cheese, and maybe some juice. That was familiar. That was what he had eaten three times a day every day for his entire life. He wasn't interested in trying something new. He just wanted what he was used to.

Mama explained this to the waiter. The waiter understood. He said the dinner Yesnir wanted was called a "typical Nicaraguan meal" and the restaurant could provide it. Mama had no idea how they did it since beans were not on the menu anywhere, but when it was time to serve the entrees, the waiter served Yesnir exactly what he was used to.

The next day Mama hired a taxi to drive her and the boys around for the day. Mama didn't know where any shops were in Managua, so she needed the expertise and recommendations of the driver to know where to go. Taking a taxi in Nicaragua could be a dangerous thing to do, so Mama took extra precautions to make sure it would be safe. Papa's good friend Kenneth, who was from Nicaragua, had taught Mama what to do.

First, rather than flagging down a taxi on the street, Mama had the hotel call a taxi for her.

Then, before getting into the taxi, Mama walked around it, giving it a quick visual inspection to make certain the driver took good care of his vehicle. He did. She took a picture of the license plate and texted it to Papa.

"May I see your driver's license please?" Mama asked the driver in Spanish. He searched through his things, found his driver's license, and handed it to her.

"Thank you," Mama said.

Mama took a picture of the license and texted it to Papa. The driver watched her do these things. Many people did this before getting into taxis in Nicaragua, so he was used to it.

Because Mama always did these things before she got into any taxi, she never had any issues with taxi drivers during any of her years in Nicaragua.

Mama and the boys went to three different home-decorating stores and the mall. They got lunch at the only restaurant at the mall that had a typical Nicaraguan lunch on its menu. Then they headed back to their hotel.

They spent the rest of the day at the pool. Anders, who could not yet swim, played on the steps, and Yesnir did endless cannon balls into the deep end. Then they started playing a game: Yesnir pretended to trip and fall into the pool. Anders watched and laughed uproariously.

"Again!" Anders said.

Yesnir did it again. Then Anders wanted him to do it again. Yesnir did it again. Then Anders wanted him to do it yet again. And so it went until Yesnir had pretended to fall in a dozen times.

Mama could see Yesnir was tired but also determined. He was in a stamina contest with Anders. Yesnir wanted to see if he could outlast Anders.

Mama smiled, enjoying the show. Everyone at some point tries to see if they can outlast a three-year-old saying "again." Mama had never seen anyone win before, but she was curious to see if Yesnir could. After all, he was young too.

By the seventeenth time, though, when Anders said "Again!" while laughing uproariously, Yesnir collapsed by the side of the pool, too tired to do it again.

"No more!" he said in Spanish. "I can't do anymore!"

Mama chuckled. How many times would a three-year-old say "again!" before getting tired of it? Mankind would ever know because no one, not even a nine-year-old, could do it enough times.

9. Sticky Fingers

For two months life continued in much same way. The well got deeper every day, but still there was just more mud and rock. Every day Anders did his workbooks, listened to Mama reading to him, dug in his dirt piles, and played with Yesnir and Jesslyn when they came over.

Moisés and Ramón began coming over every day, too. Moisés was eleven years old and Ramón was ten. Yesnir was ten now too. Yesnir's family's farm was across the highway from Anders's family's farm. Next to Yesnir's family's farm was a small schoolhouse where the local children attended school. On the other side of the schoolhouse was the farm where Moisés and Ramón lived.

Moisés and Ramón were not kind and responsible like Yesnir was. They were rambunctious and mischievous. They did not have good manners, and their family was not well liked in the neighborhood. But Anders enjoyed playing with them, so Mama naively welcomed them to the farm.

Mama naively welcomed all visitors to the farm. There was their neighbor Trinio, who stopped by to see if Mama could help him become an American citizen. There was Octavio, another neighbor, who was always drunk. He stopped by regularly to sell eggs. There was Pablo who sold fruit and vegetables out of the back of his pickup truck. He stopped by every Sunday. There were other people from the area who stopped by just once, to meet the newcomers and see what they were up to. Every time someone came over, Mama and Anders took time to meet them.

Mama and Anders made many more trips to Managua. Now they always brought another boy with them in addition to Yesnir. Sometimes Ramón came and sometimes Moisés came, but Yesnir came every time, because he was Anders's best friend.

Mama bought school supplies and swimming trunks for Moisés and Ramón too. She also bought games she thought the older boys would enjoy playing—Monopoly, Clue, and Uno were all huge hits. It was a happy time at the farm. Mama loved being a fairy godmother.

"You know they're not really going to use the stuff you bought them," James told Mama. "They're just going to sell it and use the money to buy chips and soda."

"You really think so?" Mama asked doubtfully.

"I know so," James said. "Not Yesnir. He's a good boy. But Moisés and Ramón, I'm sure. They're brats. They've got sticky fingers too."

"What do you mean?" Mama asked.

"I mean that quite a few things have been going missing from the kitchen—cups, spoons, forks, lighters, pads of paper, pens, pencils.... They're taking stuff," James said.

"No way," Mama said. "Moisés and Ramón are a little rough around the edges, it's true, but that does not mean they are thieves. The rancho only has three walls. Anyone could come onto the property at night and take stuff."

James laughed. He knew he was right, but he also knew Mama wasn't ready to hear it

"No one is coming here at night. Brava would bark," he said.

Mama sighed.

"I hope it's not Moisés and Ramón. They're our friends...."

Mama talked to Moisés and Ramón about stealing. They didn't speak English and her Spanish wasn't good enough to have conversations about psychology, but she tried to explain to them that stealing would ruin their lives, not because they might get caught and have terrible consequences (though that was true too), but because of the psychological effects of taking what you don't earn.

"Your brain knows when you do something wrong," she said. "You will secretly hate yourself. And you will make bad things happen to yourself as a punishment. Even if no one ever finds out. You will know, and you will trip and fall and hurt your knee or bang your head or get caught doing something else— you will make sure you pay for your wrongdoing. Even worse, you will lose your self-esteem. You will not fight for what you want in life. You will not work hard because you will not think you deserve it."

The boys stared at Mama. She sighed. Expressing herself in Spanish was so hard. Did they have any idea what she was trying to say? Was she even using the right words?

"We don't steal," they both said.

"Good," Mama said. "I like you guys, and I want to be your friend. But I can't be your friend if you steal."

10. If You Can't Protect It

The farm had a creek that ran through it for six months of the year. Papa dammed up part of the creek by putting in a cement wall. This created a large pool of water about ten feet deep. The pool of water in the dam lasted a few months into the dry season. This enabled Nate to get buckets of water from the dam and bring it to plants that would otherwise die from lack of water.

Watering plants with buckets of water from the dam took too long. So, on his last trip to the farm, Papa had brought a water pump from the United States. He put the pump in the dam, and then he and Nate put in pipes to bring the water from the creek to different areas of the farm. They also put in a line of pipes to the Rancho. Water brought from the dam to the Rancho could be purified and used for bathing and for Anders's little swimming pool.

Moisés and Ramón's sister stopped by one day to see if she could wash her family's laundry in the dam. Mama said she could. A few weeks later the water pump was stolen out of the dam.

"Now the plants will die," Papa said sadly on the phone when he heard the news. "Watering with buckets is just too inefficient. There is no way to get water to all the plants that need it that way."

"How expensive was the pump?" Mama asked.

"Hundreds of dollars. But that's not the hardest part," Papa said. "I brought it from the United States. We can't replace it until my next trip down."

Mama talked to Max about the stolen pump. He didn't know anything about it, but he thought it was insane that Papa and Mama kept an expensive piece of equipment, unguarded, in the dam where they let their neighbors do their laundry.

Mama talked to Erick who had come to do a wood working project at the farm. Mama had hired Erick the year before to build a door, and Erick did good work. But he also did something that none of the other Nicaraguans did—when Erick spoke with Mama, he spoke slowly; he enunciated his words, and he used simple words.

Mama found communicating in Spanish with most of the people in Nicaragua to be difficult. She was always asking them to speak slower or repeat what they had said. Talking to Erick was different. It was easy. For this reason, Mama enjoyed talking to Erick and always asked his opinion about things.

In the case of the theft, Erick recommended that Mama have him do an investigation. Mama said that sounded like a great idea, so Erick spent the next few days visiting all the neighbors and talking to them. Then he gave Mama his report.

"It was Moisés and Ramón's family that stole the pump," he said.

"Why?" Mama asked.

"They are a bad family. They don't go to church," Erick said. "One of them was arrested for stealing ten years ago, so your neighbors know they are thieves."

Mama—still too naïve to see the obvious—did not know what to think. One member of Moisés and Ramón's family was caught stealing a long time ago, now the whole family was thought of as thieves. Was it because they *were* thieves and were only caught that one time? Or was that a one-time thing done by *one* family member and now the whole family was unfairly blamed for anything that went missing in the neighborhood? If one member of their family had stolen something once, was that any reason to assume the *entire* family was a family of thieves?

Statistically… yes. Social ills are contagious and rarely exist in a vacuum. If one member of a family engages in immoral behavior, it is not certain that the others do, but it is more likely. But Mama didn't know this at the time. At the time she believed that Moisés and Ramón and her neighbors were her friends and would therefore not steal from her. She convinced herself that a stranger had stolen the pump. Mama had a lot to learn about Nicaragua.

Mama and Erick talked for a while longer. Finally, Erick said something that got through to Mama:

"Here, if you can't protect it, you don't own it," Erick explained. "No one feels bad about stealing your things. No one feels bad for you if you get robbed. If you get robbed, it's your fault for not being careful. If you get robbed, you deserved it."

Mama repeated these words to Papa later on the phone.

"If we can't protect it, we don't own it," Papa repeated.

"He says the farm should never be left alone, not for one minute," Mama said. "He says we should have a security guard."

Papa did the math.

"A security guard would cost far more than the stuff that has been stolen from us," he said. "It doesn't pencil. But let's add security to Nate's job as the farm manager. He should make sure that the farm is never left alone. If he can't be there, James should be there, and vice versa."

Later Papa and Mama would realize this was a terrible way to live. They would realize that no one can get anything done if they live in such an immoral society that houses had to be babysat at all times. They would realize that a society cannot become peaceful and prosperous if stealing is condoned in any way. They would realize that what they had been taught in school was wrong: it was not poverty that caused crime but rather crime that caused poverty.

But that was later. Right now, Papa and Mama believed that poor countries were poor because they were victims of rich countries, and poor people were poor because they lacked opportunity, not moral values, so, instead of taking Erick's advice and keeping Moisés and Ramón's family off their property, Papa and Mama decided to never let the farm be left alone and to offer Moisés, Ramón, and their sister jobs. (The jobs did not work out as neither Moisés nor Ramón nor their sister wanted jobs despite their poverty.)

A few years later Erick would hire a truck driver to do some deliveries for the farm, and in casual conversation the truck driver would mention that he had once delivered a water pump to Costa Rica for Ramón's uncle right around the time the water pump was stolen from the farm.

11. Papa Is a Hero

Mama and Anders were eating lunch in the rancho. They were having rice, beans, and tortillas. Anders was having his with mustard. For the past few months Anders had eaten everything with mustard. He was eating so much mustard that he went through more than one jar of it every week. Mama did not know why he liked mustard so much right now, or for how long he would like mustard this much, but she trusted that there was something in mustard that his body needed. So, she bought him as much mustard as he wanted to eat.[3]

"Do you want some?" Anders asked her, holding out the jar of yellow mustard after covering his rice and beans in a thick layer.

"No," Mama said. "I love mustard, but not with rice and beans." Anders shrugged and began eating.

Nate came lumbering in from the jungle to join them for lunch. He was dripping with sweat. He had just been all the way at the top of the mountain, the highest and farthest point of the property.

---

[3] Anders ate an incredible amount of mustard for about eight months when he was three years old. He did not eat it again for the rest of his childhood.

"Hey Roz," he said. "Tom sent me a message for you to call him."

"Okay," Mama said.

The only cell reception on the farm was at the top of the mountain. A great deal of bushwhacking and climbing was required to get there, which was something Mama was not willing to do, but something Nate did almost every day for one reason or another. So, if Papa needed to get ahold of Mama right away, he sent the message through Nate.

After lunch, Mama drove the car a few miles from the farm to where she was able to get a good signal for her cell phone. Then she called Papa.

"I have some big news that is not good," Papa said immediately.

"Oh my gosh, what happened?" Mama asked.

"Joe burned down our kitchen," Papa explained.

A few months back, Papa and Mama had rented the guest room of their house in Los Angeles to Anders's babysitter, a twenty-year-old from Mexico named Maria, and her boyfriend, Joe.

"How did it happen?" Mama asked.

"You remember how Joe liked to cook?" Papa asked.

"Yes," Mama said.

"Well, he was making French fries yesterday, and he came outside to tell me something. We were talking, and then we heard Maria screaming in the house. Joe went in to check on her. Then, I decided to go in too because the screams sounded serious. When I went in, the entire kitchen was on fire, and Maria and Joe were standing there, staring at it, frozen in horror," Papa said.

"Wow," Mama said.

"I grabbed the fire extinguisher and put the fire out. About five minutes later, firemen showed up. They confirmed the fire was completely out, and they gutted the kitchen. They said the fire was two inches from the attic space, and if it had hit the attic, the whole house would have been lost. If it had burned two more seconds, it would have hit the attic. I got it just time. But... we have no kitchen," Papa said.

"And you're okay? Everyone is okay?" Mama asked.

"We're all fine, though I think I am little traumatized," Papa said. "Maria and Joe probably are too. They have gone to stay with Maria's parents. They want to move out as soon as possible. They don't want to live somewhere that doesn't have a kitchen."

"That makes sense," Mama said. "I think that's for the best." Mama thought for a moment. "We have fire insurance, right?" she asked.

"Yes, of course," Papa said. "But it's going to take a while to rebuild the kitchen and jump through all the hoops. For now, it's just a lot of paperwork. Which brings me to why I wanted to talk to you right away. I need you and Anders to come back to Los Angeles as soon as possible. Someone needs to oversee the construction of the kitchen and all the phone calls and stuff from the insurance company. I am too busy at work right now, and you will want to design the new kitchen anyway, right?"

"Of course," Mama said. "That is definitely my area."

"Well, when is the earliest you can be back?" Papa asked.

"Tomorrow," Mama said, trying to digest the huge change in plans.

Papa and Mama talked a while longer, and then Mama went back to the farm. She told Anders what had happened. He looked serious.

"Papa is a hero," Anders said.

"He is," Mama agreed.

"Are the firemen still at our house?" Anders asked.

"No," Mama said. "The fire was put out before they got there. But they helped clean up, and then they went back to the fire station. Papa wants us to come back to Los Angeles right away to deal with the kitchen. The house has no kitchen right now, so we must build a new one."

"No kitchen?!" Anders exclaimed.

"No, and the walls are all damaged from the smoke and the ceiling is black from the smoke." Mama said.

"I want to see it!" Anders said. "It's a real burned down kitchen in real life!"

"Yes," Mama said.

"Can we go back to Los Angeles right now?" Anders inquired.

"We can't go back right now, but Papa is going to get us the first plane tickets he can, so maybe tomorrow but probably this weekend." Mama said.

"Okay," Anders said. He looked upset. "I am so jealous of Papa that he got to see a real fireman!"

"Oh Anders," Mama said. "That makes sense. You love firemen so much. I bet you would have loved a chance to see them in real life."

"Yes," Anders said. "And to be a hero! I wanted to put out the fire!"

"Do you need a hug?" Mama asked.

"No," Anders said, crossing his arms and looking upset.

"I'm feeling stress hormones in my body too," Mama said. "Do you remember the things that are good to do if we feel stress?"

"No," Anders said, glaring at Mama.

"We can run," Mama said, "or take deep breaths, or laugh, or cry, or hug someone, or pet a dog. Do any of those things sound good to you?"

Anders thought about this for a minute. Then, without a word, he started running. He did a lap around the rancho. Brava, the dog, got up from where she was lying and ran with him. Then Mama decided that she should run too, so she followed them. Anders stopped running for a second. He reached out his hand and touched Brava on the head.

71

"Tag, you're it!" he said. Then he ran away from her as fast as he could. Brava got excited and tore after him. Her tongue was hanging out of her mouth. She looked happy and excited. She quickly caught up to him.

Anders turned around and ran in the opposite direction. He saw Mama.

"Mama!" he exclaimed.

Mama stopped running and opened her arms wide. She thought Anders was going to jump into them. But, instead, he ran up to her, tagged her, and said, "You're it!"

Then he ran from Mama as fast as he could. Mama chased him. Anders was smiling. He was feeling better. Mama was feeling better too.

12. No Good Options

Now Mama and Anders were back in Los Angeles. They were at their house on Archwood Street, inspecting the damage the fire had done to the kitchen.

They were expecting to see burned cupboards and charred appliances. Instead, they found... nothing. The kitchen was completely gone. There were no cupboards, counters, or appliances. All their kitchen stuff was gone too—the plates, cups, silverware, blender, and worst of all, Mama's cookbooks with all her notes in them.

The walls that defined the large, open kitchen, dining, and living room area were still there on three sides. On the fourth side, where the stove had been, there was just plywood. There was no floor, just the cement foundation of the house. The ceiling was still there, but it was a dingy, gray color from the smoke.

"Wow," Mama said when she saw it.

"Wow," Anders said too.

"Where is all of our stuff?" Mama inquired.

"The insurance company sent a fire repair company. They took everything. It must be cleaned. It all has smoke damage," Papa explained.

"Wow," Mama said again, walking through the house. It was as if they had never moved in. There were no bookcases full of books, no beds—no furniture of any kind—and no clothes.

"It'll all be back in a few days," Papa said. "The insurance company will put us up at a hotel if you don't want to stay here, but it's not a nice hotel. I stayed there a few nights, but it smelled so bad, I decided I would rather be here. Luckily our box of camping supplies was in the garage, so it didn't get any fire damage so… I've been camping in the bedroom."

They walked into the bedroom. It was completely devoid of furniture. The large plastic tub where they kept their camping supplies was in one corner of the room. A sleeping bag was on the carpet with a thin sleeping pad under it.

"I just camped at our farm in Nicaragua for two months," Mama said. "Now it's time to camp in Los Angeles…." She sighed.

"Our life is hard right now," Papa said. "But we're tough. We'll get through it."

Mama nodded.

"We are healthy, and our family is together. That's all that matters," she said.

"Papa, where was the fire?" Anders asked.

"Come with me, Anders. I will give you a play-by-play," Papa said.

"Okay!" said Anders excitedly.

Papa took Anders behind the garage near the back gate of the property. He walked Anders through the experience of the fire, where he had walked and where he had stood with the fire extinguisher.

"And then the firemen came, woo, woo, woo," Anders added.

"Yes," Papa said. "The fire was already out, but the kitchen was a mess. They had axes and crowbars and just started removing everything that had been damaged."

"They did an impeccable job," Mama said.

"Yeah, they knew what they were doing," Papa agreed.

Mama and Anders drove to the hotel that the insurance company had offered to pay for. Both Papa and the reviews on the internet had said it was pretty bad, but just to make sure, Mama and Anders drove there to check it out.

Unfortunately, it was as bad as Papa and the reviews had said. Mama was sad.

"There are no good options," she said to Anders. "Just grit our teeth and get through it."

"It's okay, Mama," Anders said. "I will cuddle you."

"We are healthy, and our family is together," Mama said again. "That is all that matters."

This would be the family's mantra for the next six months.

Papa and Mama thought their only choices were to camp in their kitchen-less house while it was under construction or to stay in the hotel their insurance company had offered to them, so they chose camping at their house during the construction, thinking it would be less miserable than living at the smelly hotel. What they didn't know was that they could have fought with their insurance company for a better hotel.

If they had complained more, someone they knew likely would have told them that. But Papa and Mama valued being tough and not complaining about things, so for the next six months, through all the mess of construction, the noise, the sawdust, the different fumes of different chemicals that were detrimental to their health, though all of it, they stayed at the house and didn't complain.

13. Can Anders Be the Boss of His Hand?

Many parts of life at the Archwood House were the same as they had always been. Mama and Anders woke each morning, made the beds—which the cleaning company had returned with the rest of the furniture—and got dressed. That was the same.

Then they made breakfast. That was different. Before, making breakfast had involved cooking. Now making breakfast only involved a bag of sprouted granola and a jug of milk. Before, breakfast had meant setting the table. Now they ate breakfast picnic-style on a picnic blanket on the carpet in the bedroom.

Before, washing up after breakfast had involved the kitchen sink; now it involved the bathroom one. Brushing their teeth after breakfast hadn't changed though. And sitting down to do some work after brushing their teeth hadn't changed either.

Next to the bed, Mama kept a basket of work for Anders to do. In the basket was a book that he was using to learn his letter sounds, a chapter book that Mama read to him, and a selection of math and logic workbooks. Each morning Anders sat at his little desk and did whatever work he felt like doing for as long as he felt like doing it, which was usually about an hour.

After workbooks it was time to work on the house. The first problem to solve was the air pollution from the fire and the construction. Papa put up a thick wall of plastic between the part of the house with the kitchen, dining, and living room area and the hallway that led to the bedrooms and bathroom. This kept the construction dust in the living area and out of the part of the house that they were currently occupying.

The air in the bedrooms still smelled terrible though, so Mama began researching air purifiers on the internet. Mama thought that buying an air purifier would be easy. She thought that she could just do a search for "best air purifier" and have one ordered in twenty minutes. But that is not what happened at all.

Mama read opinion after opinion about what the best air purifier was and why. There were so many different opinions. There were so many different options.

"Anders," Mama said, "this is going to take all day."

"Okay," Anders said. He went outside to play.

Mama read about HEPA filters, activated carbon, photo electrochemical oxidation, ultra-low-particle air, UV filters, ionic filters, ozone filters, and disinfecting filtration systems.

After playing for a long time, Anders came back inside.

"What are you doing, Mama?" he asked.

"I am *still* reading about air purifiers," Mama said. "But I have found this website called AbundantEarth.com that looks trustworthy, so I am going to call them. Do you want to dial the number for me?"

"Yes!" said Anders.

Mama handed her phone to Anders and read him the numbers one at a time. He pressed them into her phone.

"Now hit the green button," Mama instructed.

Anders did, and the phone started ringing. Mama put it on speakerphone, so Anders could listen to the call.

"Abundant Earth. This is Brian," a pleasant-sounding, male voice answered.

"Oh wow," Mama said, "I was not expecting to get a person! I was expecting to get, 'Press five to talk to a sales representative,' or something. How wonderful to have a real person answer the phone!"

Brian laughed.

"How can I help you?" he asked.

"I need to buy an air purifier and was wondering if I could ask you some questions," Mama said.

"Of course," Brian said. "Ask away."

Mama started asking Brian her questions. She had many questions. Brian patiently talked to her explaining why Abundant Earth recommended the air purifiers they did. Mama could not believe her luck. He was knowledgeable and able to break things down and explain them to her in a simple way. Anders, however, found the phone call boring and went back outside.

Forty-five minutes later Mama came outside. Anders was playing a game with his construction trucks.

"I ordered the air purifier!" Mama said.

Anders stopped what he was doing and glared at Mama. He raised his right arm back.

"Uh oh, Anders!" Mama said. "It looks like your arm wants to hit me! Can you be the boss of it, or do you need help?"

"I can be the boss!" Anders said.

"Okay, then use your other hand to stop that one!" Mama said urgently. Anders grabbed his right arm with his left hand and held it close to his body.

"Now say, 'I'm not going to let you hit anyone. I am the boss,'" Mama instructed.

Anders looked at his arm and spoke sternly, "I'm not going to let you hit. I am the boss," he said.

"Wow, Anders!" Mama said. "I am so impressed! You did that so well that I thought you were a five-year-old!"

"Yeah," Anders said, beaming. "I am like a five-year-old."

"Do you know why your arm wanted to hit me?" Mama asked.

"No," Anders said.

"Was it because I interrupted you?" Mama asked.

"No," Anders said. Then he realized why he felt angry. "It was because you took so long!"

"Oh," Mama said gravely. "That makes sense. You have been waiting and waiting for me to be done all day."

"Yes, I have been waiting and waiting!" Anders said.

"Waiting is hard," Mama agreed. "I'm done now though. Do you want to go to a restaurant and get some lunch?"

"Yes," Anders said. "My stomach says it is suuuper hungry."

"My stomach is super hungry too," Mama said. "In fact, I don't know if I can even wait until I get to a restaurant. I think I am going to have to have you for lunch!"

Mama's eyes were big, and she looked serious as she took one of Anders's arms and brought it to her mouth.

"I bet you taste like chicken," she said.

"No, don't eat me!" Anders exclaimed.

"You better run then," Mama said. "Maybe run and hide from me in the car! But with your seatbelt on, so we can leave right away!"

Anders ran to the car. He climbed into his car seat and buckled it all by himself as he usually did. Mama ran after him, nibbled his arm a few more times, and then tightened his car-seat harness and closed the door.

The air purifier arrived in the mail a few days later. It had a light on it that indicated the air quality of the room that it was in. The light was green when the air quality was good, yellow when it was medium, and red when it was bad.

When Mama first turned the air purifier on, the light was red for a week. But then the light turned yellow and, eventually, green.

14. Restaurant Regulars

Many parts of life were the same as they had always been. Each day at noon Mama and Anders ate lunch. That was the same.

Before the fire, they had made lunch and eaten it at their house. Now they went out for lunch most days. It was fun at first, but Mama and Anders quickly tired of restaurant food. There was one good thing about eating out a lot though—they became regulars at several different restaurants.

Their favorite restaurant was called the Peasant Wine Bistro. They ate there three to five days a week. Anders always got the fish, the chicken, or the steak. Mama always got one of their soups or salads. Mama and Anders dined there so often that the cook came out to meet them, and then the owner did as well. The waiters even took Anders back to see the kitchen and often gave him a free dessert.

"This is amazing," Mama said. "I always liked going to different restaurants and trying new things, but the secret to a good life is actually eating at the same place and becoming a regular. It's so wonderful to come and say 'hi' to our friends, and for them to know us and what we like!"

Anders sat down at their usual table.

"Ock ock," he said, agreeing with Mama.

"Zock mock yock," Mama said, pretending that she understood what Anders had said and was replying.

Anders giggled.

"Ooosh kooshi bash mash roosh?" Mama asked, looking right at Anders and acting as if she were saying real words.

"Osshi booshi," Anders said, giggling.

"Bash, bash," Mama said. "Gargly moogly tookly bookly."

Mama made her eyes big and nodded her head as if she were telling Anders something really interesting.

Anders cracked up.

"What are you saying, Mama?" he inquired.

"Nothing really. I'm pretending that I have something really interesting to say," Mama explained.

"Let's use real words now," Anders said.

"Okay," Mama said. "Should we talk about what we want to order today?"

"Yes," Anders said.

Just then the waiter, Chris, appeared with a plate of food.

"Chef is thinking of offering this as the special today. Do you guys want to taste it and tell us what you think?" Chris asked.

"Yes!" Anders said.

Chris put the plate of food down.

After lunch most days Mama and Anders went to a home improvement store or two. They did this every day for weeks while they debated the different choices that needed to be made for the new kitchen.

There were so many choices to be made: What color should the walls be? Should the ceiling be the same color or a different color? Should the walls be textured or flat? Should the ceiling be textured or flat? Should the paint be glossy or matte or in-between? What kind of lights did they want? How many? Where should each light go? How many light switches? How many electrical outlets? What kind of sink? How big? What kind of faucet? Gas oven or electric oven? What kind of floor? What color?

It was a little overwhelming.

Anders helped as much as he could. He spent hours with Mama at lighting stores, cupboard stores, countertop stores, appliance stores, flooring stores, and hardware stores. They got samples and spent hours looking at different combinations of floor options, with paint color options, and countertop options. It was a lot of work.

In Nicaragua the well digging happened slowly, a little bit every day. In Los Angeles, building the kitchen happened in fits and starts. One day, an attic company came. They replaced the old insulation in the attic with new insulation. Then, nothing happened for several weeks until the drywall people came. Then the drywall people came and in one day rebuilt the wall. Then nothing happened for several weeks. Then the painters came. In one day, they painted the ceiling white and the walls the color Mama and Anders had chosen, a warm white with a hint of rose. Then it was back to waiting for the next vendor.

Anders did not enjoy the building process in Los Angeles. He waited for each vendor with the excitement and enthusiasm with which he waited for his birthday, but vendor after vendor turned out to be a frustrating experience.

"Why don't they give me any work to do?" Anders asked. "Why don't they let me help? Why do they tell me to go away?"

"I don't know, Anders," Mama said. "The culture here is different. Maybe it's because they are afraid of lawsuits if you got hurt, or maybe they are so used to children being shut up in school that they don't know how to include them in life."

Mama thought for a minute.

Then she said, "I have work you can help me with if you want. The patio could really use some sweeping. We can have a contest to see if you can put things away faster than I can sweep. And then when everything is put away, I can pretend that I think I need to sweep you up!"

"Okay," Anders said smiling and heading outside. He loved it when Mama tried to sweep him up.

15. Running in Parking Lots

Now it was time to go to the grocery store. Mama went outside to where Anders was digging.

"Hello young man!" Mama said.

"Hello old lady!" Anders said.

Mama chuckled.

"I need to go buy some groceries. Would you like to come with me?" Mama asked.

"Yes!" Anders said. Wherever Mama was going, Anders always wanted to go too.

When they got to the grocery store, Anders made a beeline for the cookies. He picked up a large cookie.

"How about you buy me this cookie? You can buy me one cookie or two cookies. You decide," he said.

"How about… no cookies," Mama said.

"But I want one!" Anders argued.

"But I don't want those cookies because they are not the kind of cookies I eat. Those have food coloring in them, and that is a chemical that I don't want in my body. How about instead we go home and make pumpkin cookies?" Mama offered.

"That's a great decision!" Anders said.

But then, after thinking about it, he changed his mind.

"But I want cookies now," he said sadly.

"Waiting is hard," Mama agreed. "Let's look around. Maybe there is something we can get right now that will make both of us happy."

Anders found lots of packaged things that would make him happy, but they did not make Mama happy. Mama found bottles of bubble water and kombucha that would make her happy, but they didn't make Anders happy. Finally, they went to the fruit section and found some watermelon that was already cut up and ready to eat. This made both of them happy.

"Anders are you a little bit hungry or very hungry?" Mama asked, trying to decide whether they should get the little thing of cut up watermelon or the big thing.

"Oh, I'm very, very, very, very, very hungry. I'm like a twelve hungry!" Anders said.

"You know what I just realized, Anders?" Mama asked, grabbing the larger container of watermelon. "It's lunch time, and we haven't had lunch. I'm so sorry. Being a twelve hungry probably doesn't feel good."

Mama thought for a moment.

"Anders, I can be so forgetful. If we are about to leave the house, and you are hungry, it would be helpful if you reminded me or got yourself a snack.

You are three, so you are old enough to know when you are hungry and be in charge of making sure you get some food," she said.

"Okay, Mama," Anders said. "I will be in charge. I can do that."

Mama paid for the watermelon, and they went outside to eat it.

Outside the store there was a wide sidewalk where there were some tables and chairs. All but two were empty. Mama and Anders sat down at a table. They ate the entire large container of watermelon.

Next to where Mama and Anders sat the sidewalk continued over a small hill about ten feet long with a total rise of about two feet; beyond this hill were other stores.

After Anders was done with his watermelon, he went to inspect the hill. He walked up the hill and then down it, always staying on the sidewalk. Then he walked up the hill and ran down it. He did that again with his arms out pretending he was an airplane. Anders thought this was great fun, so he did it several more times, never once leaving the sidewalk.

The people at the tables nearby stared at Anders as if he were doing something terribly dangerous. Mama felt annoyed. It was a slow day at the store. There were no cars moving anywhere nearby, and Anders, running down the sidewalk, was clearly interested in exploring the hill, not randomly running around.

Mama watched Anders with a smile, completely ignoring the looks she was getting from the people at the tables. An older woman from one of the tables approached her.

"Your little boy is going to run into the parking lot," the woman said.

Mama smiled pleasantly at the woman.

"I don't think so," Mama said. "He has never done anything like that before."

Then, before the woman could say something else, Mama called out, "Anders, are you going to run out into the parking lot?"

Anders stopped what he was doing and looked at Mama like she was nuts.

"No," he said. "You run in the parking lot you could die. That's for stupid people. It's not for me."

Mama looked at the woman. She thought maybe the woman would laugh delightedly at Anders's answer, but instead the woman looked shocked and annoyed.

"I've drilled the dangers of parking lots into his head since he was a toddler," Mama offered. "Car accidents are the leading cause of death for kids his age. Half the people that die in car accidents are not inside a car. Being a pedestrian around cars is the most dangerous thing we do; the number one way he could die. He knows. He always asks for someone to hold his hand or carry him before he goes into a parking lot or a road. He's super cautious…."

The woman did not look impressed or even appeased. She just looked more annoyed. Mama tried again to connect with her.

"I know not all kids are like Anders. Thank you so much for trying to keep him safe," she said.

The woman didn't say anything. She just walked away. Mama sighed.

"Anders," Mama said, going to him, "these people can't handle seeing you run back and forth like that. They're freaking out. Do you think we can meet their needs, so they can stop being worried? Can we finish our shopping?"

"You choose, Mama. Whatever you want is fine with me!" Anders said.

"Let's finish shopping," Mama said.

"Okay, Mama," Anders agreed.

As they were heading back into the grocery store Mama said, "I am so glad I don't have to worry about you around cars, Anders. I feel so happy to have a son like you."

"Yeah, you wouldn't want a son that runs around cars and gets dead," Anders agreed. "I don't want that son either."

16. Truman's Favorite Chips

Now a Renaissance fair was happening near Los Angeles. Mama went outside to get Anders. He was playing with a toy car. He had built a road out of mud and was driving the car and talking to himself. Mama did not interrupt him right away. First, she watched his game.

"Drive… now turn right… on the freeway… proceed to the route! Proceed to the route!"

Mama chuckled. Anders had heard her map app say "proceed to the route" so many times, he had made it part of his game.

"Hey Mama," Anders said.

"Hey Anders," Mama said, "it's time to get ready to go to the Renaissance fair. Can you come in now and get cleaned up?"

"Yes!" Anders said, hopping up and leaving his toys behind him.

"Do you remember that your friend Truman is going to come with us today to the fair?" Mama asked.

"I am so happy Truman is coming!" Anders said gleefully dancing around. "Do you know what I am planning to show Truman at the Renaissance fair?" Anders asked.

He told Mama his plans while they walked inside. Mama was thinking about something else, so she didn't hear what Anders said.

"Isn't that a good idea?" Anders asked.

"Can you tell me again, Anders, I wasn't listening," Mama said apologetically.

Anders thought for a moment.

Then he said, "I can't! My body deleted it. I can only tell you one time."

"I'm so sorry Anders. Listening is such an important skill. I will do better," Mama said.

Soon Mama, Anders, and Truman were in the car on their way to the Renaissance fair.

"Mama, I can't reach the chips," Anders said.

"What chips?" Mama asked.

"The chips for Truman. Right there," Anders said, pointing behind Mama's seat.

Mama was dubious. She hadn't put any chips in the car. In fact, she hadn't packed any snacks for the boys. Nevertheless, she reached behind her seat to where Anders was pointing. Sure enough, there was a full, unopened bag of organic potato chips cooked in coconut oil—a kind of chips Truman had expressed a great liking for the last time he visited Anders. Mama couldn't believe it. How did these chips get into the car? She opened the chips and handed them back to Anders.

"Here Truman, have some," Anders said, passing the bag to Truman.

"Thanks, Anders!" Truman said. Truman took a large handful.

"Anders, did you put those chips in the car?" Mama asked.

"Yeah," Anders said.

"Because you remembered how much Truman liked them last week?" Mama asked.

"Yeah," Anders said.

"That was so thoughtful of you!" Mama exclaimed.

"Yeah," Anders agreed. "Cause I'm big. I'm so thoughtful. I'm like six!"

Soon they were at the Renaissance faire. Mama bought their tickets, and they went inside. At the front of the fair were historical booths. Anders and Truman stopped for a long time to watch women spin wool on spinning wheels. Then they watched blacksmiths pound red-hot metal into tools. Then they continued walking along the fair's dirt road.

On both sides of the dirt road were shops and activities. There was a lot to see and do. There were shops with beautiful, artisanal bracelets, crowns made of flowers, clothing, toys, and goblets. There were real, metal swords and knives. There were stages where people sang, told jokes, and did all kinds of shows.

The boys sat for a while on some hay bales and watched a man with a large, majestic bird, called a hawk. He had trained the bird so that it could fly fast through the air and catch things that he threw. The boys were impressed.

They continued walking through the fair, past booths that sold watermelon, lemonade, and toasted nuts. One booth sold meat pies that smelled tasty.

"Are you guys hungry?" Mama asked.

"Yeah," Truman said.

"Yes," Anders said.

Mama bought a few meat pies and some bottles of waters, and the three of them sat down on nearby hay bales for a snack.

When Anders was done eating, he remembered the boys he had seen jumping from hay bale to hay bale the year before and decided to see if this year he could do it. He was much bigger this year than he was last year, after all.

Anders climbed onto a haybale and then, standing, approached the edge. He judged the distance to the next hay bale as something he could step across. He focused and then acted—he reached out with his right foot and made a small jump. He made it!

Anders walked to the edge of the hay bale he was on now and again stopped, focused, and jumped to the next hay bale. Again, he made it!

Now Anders was feeling more confident and started going faster and faster from one hay bale to the next. He did the whole row of them—twelve hay bales!

Truman watched Anders and decided he was not ready to do any jumping from hay bale to hay bale, but he did enjoy running up and down the long rows of hay bales, just as Anders had the year before.

At one end of the twelve rows of hay bales was a stage where performances were held throughout the day. No one was on the stage right now. Anders looked at it curiously. There was a stone bench in the middle of the stage. He wanted to sit there.

"Truman!" he called. "Come see this!"

Truman climbed down from the hay bale he was on and walked up the center aisle to where Anders was. Anders stood at the bottom of three small stairs that went to the stage.

"Come on Truman. Let's go up there!" Anders said.

"I don't want to," Truman said, shying away from the stage

Anders watched him for a minute, unsure of what he should do. Then he made up his mind.

He climbed the stairs onto the stage, went to the stone bench in the middle, and took a seat.

Anders looked out over the haybales. There were a few families sitting here and there resting or eating. There was his Mama—he smiled at her. And there was Truman. Truman sat on one of the hay bales in the front row watching Anders.

Anders looked around for a while, imagining something. He smiled. Then he got off the bench and climbed down from the stage.

Mama was impressed with how the boys had solved their problem. Each boy was confident enough to do what he wanted to do. Neither one pressured the other to be different.

"What were you imagining up there?" Mama asked Anders when he came down.

"That everyone was clapping for me and laughing so hard," Anders said gleefully, "because I farted so big!"

17. Montessori and Cleaning the Pool

Now it was evening. Mama had spent several hours researching ovens online and was close to deciding which one to buy. Anders was playing out back. The front door opened and in walked Papa. Mama stopped what she was doing and gave Papa a big hug.

"How was your day?" she asked.

"Long," Papa answered. "Yours?"

"Also long," Mama said.

"Where's Anders?" Papa asked.

"In the backyard," Mama answered.

"How did the preschool tour go?" Papa asked.

Mama and Anders had toured their sixth Montessori preschool earlier.

"Not great," Mama said. "I like Montessori education in theory. I love her books, but I am completely unimpressed with these schools. They are so ugly—gates and fences everywhere. They look like prisons. I walk inside the building and already feel the life being sucked out of me by the sheer ugliness of it all."

Mama had been reading Christopher Alexander's books on objective beauty in architecture. She agreed with Alexander that beautiful spaces energized and motivated people, and ugly ones drained people of energy and demotivated them.

"Was this one more faithful to Montessori's ideas than the last ones?" Papa asked.

"No. This was the best one we have toured yet, but they separated the kids, so the three-year-olds weren't in the same classroom as the four-year-olds—that's not Montessori. Their puzzles were multi-colored—that is not Montessori. And they also read fiction to the kids—that's not Montessori either."

"Do you still think Anders needs some years of Montessori preschool as part of his education?" Papa asked.

"Yes and no," Mama said. "I still want him to do some Montessori math, but I watched the kids at the school for thirty minutes, and… maybe Montessori is the best option if your kid must go to preschool, but being at home with Mom is better. Anders was more advanced than the kids at the school."

"It would make sense. Life offers more educational opportunities than school," Papa said.

"I'm not into him hanging out with a bunch of other three-year-olds all day. In the real world, kids act so much better. The three-year-olds try to act like the seven-year-olds, who are trying to like the fifteen-year-olds, who are trying to act like the adults. When you take a bunch of three-year-olds and put them in a pen with other three-year-olds… they devolve or something. Three-year-olds who hang out with three-year-olds all day talk like babies. Anders talks like an adult. Or at least a six-year-old."

"Keep him home," Papa said.

Mama nodded.

"I talked to the preschool about sending him there for an hour a few times a week for math tutoring. I can give up the rest of the Montessori education, but I really like the concrete math. I think that would be the best option," Mama said.

"That sounds good," Papa agreed.

Papa went outside to see Anders. Anders was sitting in one of the chairs on the patio playing with a construction truck.

"I am so tired from my long day at work," Papa said loudly, pretending he did not see Anders. "I just need to sit down and relax for a minute."

Papa sat on top of Anders. Anders giggled.

"Oh, this chair is so soft and warm," Papa said, adjusting his position. "But this pillow is a little lumpy."

Papa scrunched Anders together as if he were a pillow. Anders giggled more.

"Ah, that's good. Now, where is my son? I would really like to see my son," Papa said while looking around.

"I'm right here, Papa!" Anders said from beneath him.

Papa sprang up.

"What! My pillow just talked to me!" he exclaimed.

Anders roared with laughter. Papa picked him up into a big hug.

"Anders! I'm so happy to see you!" Papa said.

They finished their hug. Papa noticed that the gate to the pool was open. He went to close it and saw a bunch of Anders's toys near the pool.

"What were you working on?" Papa asked Anders.

"A big construction project," Anders said.

Anders had been having his construction trucks pick up piles of dirt, drive the long distance over the patio to the pool, and... dump the dirt into the pool. There was a small pile of dirt on the pool steps, and the water near it looked murky.

"Anders," Papa said, approaching Anders and kneeling down to his eye level. "I am feeling upset about the dirt you put in the pool."

"Oh," Anders said, looking at what he had done. "How about, next time, I never put a lot of dirt in the pool ever again—just a little!" Anders said.

"That does not work for me," Papa said. "I don't want you to put *any* dirt in the pool."

Anders thought for a moment.

"How about... I'll make a big surprise for you! I'll trade you—next time I go to the hair salon, I'll get you soooo many candies," Anders offered.

"Anders, I like how you are thinking about this problem, but a trade will not work for me this time. When you put dirt in the pool, it makes extra work for me. I am a busy guy. I don't want extra work. I want you to help me have less work, not more work. I don't want *any* dirt in the pool," Papa said.

Anders understood.

"How about, next time, I never put any dirt in the pool ever again?" he offered.

"Anders, if you would be willing to do that, I would appreciate it. Your consideration for my needs would make me feel happy. A considerate family is the kind of family I would be happy to have."

"Yes," said Anders. "That's my family."

"Now we need to get out the pool vacuum and clean the pool," Papa said.

"Okay," said Anders. "And then wrestling time?"

Normally after work Papa and Anders had a fun, high-energy wrestling session.

"I'm afraid we won't be able to wrestle today, Anders. Cleaning up the pool is going to take all our wrestling time. But we can wrestle tomorrow," Papa said.

"But we are supposed to wrestle right now," Anders said. "You said when you got home, we would wrestle!"

"Our plans must change because you put dirt in the pool, and we must deal with that now. I'm sad that you put dirt in the pool, and we don't get to wrestle, but that's the choice you made. I hope you will choose differently tomorrow. Now, your job, because you made a mess, is to help me clean it up. Then we need to talk about pool safety and what you should do next time if you find the gate open," Papa said.

"Okay," Anders said sadly.

"Clean up, clean up, everyone everywhere," Papa began singing.

Anders joined in and they sang together as Papa got out the pool vacuum, "Clean up, clean up, everyone—do your share. Many hands make the work so light. Everybody helping—that's doing it right!"

18. Kylie and Rees

When Anders was a little over one year old Papa and Mama made a video that they put on the internet called, "How to NOT Treat Children." It was a comedic video in which Papa treated Mama, an adult, the same way that adults treat children—he constantly interrupted her when she was talking to correct her; he reminded her to share; when she complained he told her that she didn't feel the way she said she felt; when she started to cry, he shoved a pacifier in her mouth; and he made her put her coat on even though she insisted that she wasn't cold.

Mama had been inspired to make the video after taking classes in respectful parenting offered by the RIE center in Los Angeles. RIE stands for *Resources for Infant Educarers.*

Sixty thousand people watched the video. Mama received emails from strangers telling her how much they enjoyed it. One of those emails was from a woman named Melanie who worked as a RIE teacher.

Melanie grew up in South Dakota, but now she lived in Los Angeles with her husband, Dave, and their four children. It turned out that Melanie's family lived only a few blocks away from Papa, Mama, and

Anders! The internet was such an incredible tool for making new friends. Mama loved it.

Now Mama and Melanie had been good friends for over a year. Melanie's eleven-year-old daughter, Kylie, was over at the house working as a mother's helper by playing with Anders while Mama finished up the design for the new kitchen. Kylie's five-year-old brother, Rees, had come too.

Rees and Anders were playing with their favorite toy—dirt. They sat in it, filled their trucks with it, drove their trucks around in it, and rubbed their hands in it. Anders buried a rock and then dug it up.

Rees liked that idea, so he buried a pile of rocks and dug them up. Anders liked that idea, so he buried a pile of rocks and then used his excavator to dig them up. Rees liked that idea, so he brought over his dump truck for Anders to put the rocks into as he dug them up. Anders turned on the hose and now some of the dirt was mud. Rees filled his dump truck with mud and drove it to the walkway where he dumped it. He imagined making a giant pile of mud there, so much mud that the walkway would be covered.

Anders realized he was thirsty and wanted a glass of water. He went to the door. Kylie instantly sprang into action. She stood in front of the door.

"I can't let you go inside, Anders," she said, "You are too muddy."

"Oh," Anders said. "I remember!"

Anders went to the hose. He used it to rinse off his feet, his legs, and his hands. Then he turned it off.

"You always have to remember to turn it off!" he reminded himself.

Anders went back to Kylie. Kylie handed him a towel. Anders wiped his hands and patted his legs dry. Then he wiped the bottom of his feet repeatedly on the mat. Finally, Kylie stepped back from the door and let him go inside.

19. The Three Little Pigs

Mama and Anders were at a restaurant sharing a fish plate. It had five different types of fish on it and a variety of breads, fruits, and pickles to enjoy with the fish.

"My favorite is the gravlax," Mama said.

"My favorite is the sardines," Anders said. "May I have all of them?"

"Sure," Mama said. "Sardines have edible bones in them—maybe your body needs to grow bigger bones right now."

"Yes, I think my body is saying that to me," said Anders.

When Mama and Anders were done eating and were waiting for the check to come, Mama pulled a book out of her purse.

"Can I read you another version of *The Three Little Pigs*?" Mama asked.

"Yes!" Anders said.

This was the twenty-third and final version of *The Three Little Pigs* Mama had borrowed from the library. She had yet to find one that she liked.

The Three Little Pigs had been one of Mama's favorite stories when she was a little girl. Mama had identified with the smart pig that worked hard and built his house out of bricks, and she had been happy that the lazy pigs got what they deserved—being eaten by the big, bad wolf. Mama had no idea what version she had read as a kid, but it did not seem to exist now. Perhaps it had never existed, and Mama had fixed the story in her mind as a child.

The Los Angeles Public Library had twenty-three versions of *The Three Little Pigs,* and in all of them the lazy pigs didn't get eaten. Instead, they went to live in the home of the hardworking pig who built his house of bricks. Mama thought this was a terrible lesson to teach children.

"Don't work hard!" the books were saying. "If you want to be lazy, go ahead. People who work hard will bail you out!"

Mama read this last version of *The Three Little Pigs* to Anders, and, yet again, the two lazy pigs were bailed out by the hardworking pig. There were no consequences for their poor choices.

"In real life," Mama explained, "in nature, the lazy pigs get eaten by the wolf."

"I know," Anders said.

"Anders, I am thinking about writing a proper version of *The Three Little Pigs* where the lazy pigs get eaten. It would be a lot of work—would you want to do that with me?"

"Yes!" Anders said excitedly.

"I would have to do lots of drafts. And I would want to read you my story again and again and again to make it better and better. Do you think you could handle that?"

"Yes!" Anders said.

For the next few months when there was no work to do on the kitchen except wait for the next vendor, Mama worked on her version of *The Three Little Pigs*, trying out draft after draft for Anders before he went to bed at night. Mama wanted the lazy pigs to get eaten, but she didn't want the story to be too scary for young children, so Anders gave her feedback night after night until she had a version that he thought was perfect.

Then Mama sent the story to some of her friends who had young children. Their kids read it and loved it too. Mama paid one of her other friends to make pictures for the book and one of her other friends to edit it. Then she published it on Amazon.

"Anders, if you were one of the little pigs, what would you build your house out of?" Mama asked Anders one day.

"Ehh... maybe straw," Anders said, shrugging.

Mama was crushed. Was Anders a fool? How could he be so irresponsible? How could he possibly identify with the straw-house pig after hearing her version of the story?

But Anders wasn't done answering.

"Or dirt," Anders said, thinking out loud. "It doesn't matter. I would have a gun. If a wolf came, I would shoot him. I always have a gun above my door."[4]

Mama laughed. Anders wasn't a fool after all.

---

[4] Anders got this idea from the *Little House* books.

20. Helping to Solve Problems

Now the kitchen was almost done. One day, after a particularly frustrating encounter with the man who was installing the sink, Anders came to Mama.

"Mama, I have no work to do, so I'm going to throw things at people and take their stuff," Anders said.

"Wow," Mama said. "It sounds like you really need some work to do."

"Yeah," Anders said, "I just have nothing to do."

"I'd like to help you solve that problem, so you don't have to be rude to people," Mama said.

"Thanks Mama," Anders said. "You always help me solve my problems."

"I think you should check with Papa to see if he has any work you could do," Mama suggested.

Anders thought that was a great idea. He found Papa in the backyard.

"Papa, do you have any work I can do?" Anders asked.

"As a matter of fact, I do," Papa said looking at his phone. "The new fridge just got here, and I need to help the delivery men. Do you want to help too?"

"Yes!" Anders said, jumping up.

Papa and Anders went outside. The front of the house had a circular driveway, so a car could park right outside the front door—that's where Papa's car was right now.

The man driving the delivery truck had pulled up behind Papa's car. If Papa moved his car, the delivery truck could get closer to the front door.

Papa hopped in his car, drove it out of the driveway, and parked it on the street. Anders directed the delivery driver, so he could park as close to the front door as possible. Then Anders directed the delivery driver and the other delivery man with him into the house. Anders showed them where to put the huge box containing the new fridge.

Once it was in place Papa opened the box. The delivery men helped Papa remove the fridge. Papa and Anders inspected it carefully. It looked perfect. Papa signed the papers, and the delivery men left.

"Papa, look at this box," Anders said. "I am so freaking excited about this box."

The box the fridge had arrived in was the size of a kid's tree house. It was huge. Anders got right to work turning it into a home.

He got a pencil and marked where the windows should be. Papa used his saw to cut window holes in the thick cardboard. Anders colored the box with markers. Then he moved the box to many different locations around the house, looking for the perfect spot for it to go. Eventually he decided it should go on the patio near his dirt piles and construction vehicles.

Anders swept the floor of his little box house and made a bed inside it with a blanket and a pillow. He brought books and toys to the box and played in there for hours.

Mama stopped by to visit him.

"I love your house," she said.

"Thank you," said Anders. "Would you like some tea?"

"Yes, of course," Mama said.

Anders got Mama a pretend cup of tea. Mama pretended to drink it.

"Why did you decide to build your house here?" Mama asked.

"My house has to go right by my factory," he said, nodding to his construction site. "I am a rich man."

"Ah," Mama said. "You are remembering the Korean proverb my friend Yumi told us about—the one that says, 'A man who lives within walking distance of his factory will become rich.' How wise you are."

Anders nodded.

"I am very wise," he said.

Just then Mama snorted.

"Ah!" she exclaimed. "A bug flew up my nose!"

21. Sunday Sugar

Now it was May. Anders was three and a half. For several weeks Mama and Anders had been landscaping one little area of their yard at a time. They had a huge yard—a quarter of an acre—so landscaping it had been quite a bit of work. With no kitchen to cook in together, gardening turned out to be the perfect activity for Mama and Anders to share. Anders loved gardening. Mama didn't, but she loved making her yard look nicer, and she loved spending productive time with her little boy.

Today Mama and Anders drove to a nursery to buy flowers to plant along the side of the house.

They parked the car in a large parking lot and entered a giant, square store filled to the brim with plants. It was warm and humid inside the nursery. The air smelled of fresh earth and flowers. The nursery had several fountains, so there was a pleasant sound of trickling water to listen to wherever Mama and Anders walked. The nursery had interesting statues for sale in addition to plants that were beautiful to see. One wall opened onto a large lot that was filled with plants that needed direct sunlight. There were even trees for sale.

"I love this nursery," Mama said looking around. "It is so lovely."

"I love this nursery too," Anders said. "I remember… they have candy!"

"They do," Mama said.

Anders pointed a pretend remote control at Mama. "I'm robot-ing you! Candy is good for you!"

Mama laughed.

"Wouldn't that be nice? I wish candy were good for us! Then we could eat it all the time," she said.

The last time Mama and Anders had been to this store, the cashier had offered Anders a piece of candy when they were checking out. In Anders's family they only ate sugary foods on Sundays, so Mama had put the piece of candy in her purse and saved it for Sunday.

"What day is it today?" Anders asked.

"Today is Monday," Mama said. "Monday, Tuesday, Wednesday, Thursday, Friday, Saturday, Sunday." Mama held up her fingers and counted while she listed off the days of the week. "It is six days until Sunday."

Anders was sad. That was many days to wait.

"Does your right-now brain want to eat the candy right now?" Mama asked.

"Yeah," Anders said.

"And what about your future brain? What does Future-Anders want?"

"He doesn't want me to eat any candy because he doesn't want any cavities," Anders said.

"Right-Now-Roslyn is the same," Mama said. "In my head Right-Now-Roslyn is throwing a fit! She wants candy right now! And she's yelling and screaming!"

Anders giggled at the thought of his Mama having a right-now brain that was throwing a fit.

"And now Future-Roslyn is talking to her and giving her a hug," Mama continued. "Future-Roslyn is saying, 'I'm so sorry you can't have the candy. I need to be healthy. If you keep me healthy then I can do such good work and have so much fun. But if you don't take care of me, and I am sick all the time, I will not be able to accomplish your goals for you. Will you please take care of me? If you take care of me, you will have such a good life!' What do you think Right-Now-Roslyn should do? Should she love Future-Roslyn and take of her?" Mama asked.

"Yes," Anders said. "Let's take care of her, but let's put a piece of candy in your purse for Sunday."

"Okay," Mama said. "When the cashier gives me a piece of candy, I will make sure to do that."

"Mama," Anders said, pensively looking at a desert garden display with sand, "how could they fit that much sand into the beach? Who's *Nature*?"

"That is a tough question, Anders," Mama said. "Nature is an abstract idea. Nature is everything about the Earth that happens naturally, without humans making it happen. Like a forest or an ocean. Humans didn't make forests and oceans. So, they are part of nature. Humans did make cities and cars, so those are not part of nature. Some people talk about nature as if it were a person. They call it 'Mother Nature.' But nature isn't really a person. Nature is an idea."

"Oh," Anders said. Then he noticed a fountain nearby. "You want to see the coolest thing you have ever seen in the world? You will be so freaking laughing about it!"

"Um, yes!" Mama said.

Anders showed Mama what he had noticed about the fountain—the water was coming out of a frog's mouth.

"That is funny," Mama said.

Mama put her finger in the stream of water.

Then she said, "Eww Anders, look what happened! This frog pretend-spat on me! Now I have pretend frog spit on my finger!"

"Ewww!" said Anders.

Then Anders wanted to do it too. He put his finger in the stream of water.

"Look! I have pretend frog spit on my finger!" he said.

"Eww!" Mama said. "Now whatever you do, don't touch with me with that finger!"

Anders giggled with glee and tried to touch his mom with his wet finger. Mama dodged him a few times but eventually he got her.

"Nooooo! Now I have frog spit on my shirt!" Mama said in mock horror. "Ewwww!"

22. Suburban Popularity and Work Parties

At home, Mama put on some music. Anders dug holes for the plants they bought while Mama carefully removed them from their pots and put them into the holes.

Then Anders put soil around them to hold them in place. He patted the soil down. Once the flowers were secure, he carefully watered them with a watering can.

"It looks really good," a woman walking a dog called from the street.

Mama and Anders turned to look at her.

"Thank you!" Mama called.

She and Anders walked over to meet the woman.

"I'm your neighbor," the woman said. "I live three houses down. I love what you're doing with your yard."

"Thank you," Mama said again.

"If you want to smell the flowers you can," Anders told her. "They are so yummy! They're yummy as a pancake!"

The woman laughed. She exchanged a few more pleasantries with Mama, and then she continued walking down the street.

She was the third person that week to tell Mama and Anders how nice the yard looked.

Mama grabbed the clippers and set about clipping the bushes in front of the house. Anders watched her for a bit. Then he came and held his hand out for the clippers.

"I am the gardener now," he said.

"Okay," Mama said, handing him the clippers.

Anders tried to clip some parts of the bush, but he was not strong enough to work the clippers, so he settled for pretending to clip the bush and then picking up branches Mama had clipped and carrying them to the trash bin. Mama watched this go on for a minute or two.

"Anders, I am going to be the gardener again," Mama said.

"I didn't understand what you said," Anders replied. "I only speak Spanish."

"How about a new game?" Mama asked. "The front door is pretend-broken. Can you be the handyman now and fix the door?" Mama asked.

"Okay!" said Anders.

He gave the clippers back to Mama and spent the next few minutes gathering his plastic tools.

Then, he carefully examined the door, looking closely at the hinges and the doorknob. He took his screwdriver and pretended to do something to the hinges. Then he turned to Mama.

"That's the wrong tool," he explained. "I need this one!"

He put his screwdriver back in his toolbox, grabbed his wrench, and went back to work on the hinges. After putting away his wrench he touched the hinges lightly with his metal hammer. Then he measured them with his tape measure. Then he went back to using his plastic screwdriver.

"It's fixed," Anders said after another ten minutes or so.

"Thank you, Anders," Mama said. "You worked hard on that!"

Anders began playing with a pile of bricks nearby while Mama finished pruning the bushes.

"I'm building a house for the chickens," Anders said. He looked up at the sky. "I guess it's going to pretend-snow today!" he said. "Got to keep them warm."

Mama smiled.

"I love pretend snow," she said.

When they were having dinner with Papa, he said, "Our yard looks amazing. You guys have done such good work."

"I know," Anders said. "Everyone keeps telling us that."

"Like half a dozen neighbors have stopped by to tell us that and introduce themselves," Mama said.

"Our yard is making us so many new friends!" Anders added excitedly.

"I had no idea that the key to suburban popularity was yard work," Mama said.

"You know what we should bring back?" Papa asked.

"What?" Mama said.

"Work parties," Papa said. "Like, instead of inviting people over to sit around and talk or play a board game, what if you invited your friends over to help you with your yardwork? They come over, they bring their kids, the grownups get work done while they chat and the kids play, eventually you're having dinner…."

"That sounds ideal," Mama said.

"You do it at your house some weekends and your friends' houses other weekends. It's like in the past when people came over to help with the harvest or slaughter a pig or something," Papa said. "You'd hang out, and get exercise, *and* get chores done. It's a win all around."

"It's a genius idea because then you could hang out more because your time together is productive," Mama said. "When I was in high school, I did a homestay with a family in Mexico, and I will never forget how the moms and their kids hung out every day. They went from house to house and did their chores together. On Wednesdays they all came to my homestay mom's house and made their tortillas for the week. The kids played and the moms did their chores together. It's a nicer way to live."

"It would be less lonely for you and Anders for sure," Papa said. "And it seems more meaningful than hanging out when your friends come over, you know? Like you're contributing to your friends' lives or giving them a gift or something."

"Let's do it," Mama said.

"What do you think, Anders?" Papa asked.

Anders wasn't listening. He was looking at the house.

"I think when I grow up, I'll be so strong I'll be able to lift up a house," he said.

"Off topic, but I'll roll with it," Papa said. "You will be strong when you grow up, Anders, but houses are too heavy. You won't be able to actually lift up a house."

"Why not?" Anders asked. "I could use a crane."

"Oh, okay, that could work," Papa agreed.

"And I'll lift it so carefully it won't even break!" Anders said. "Papa, how could that crane truck get imagined by somebody?"

"Someone had a problem to solve. People imagine amazing things to solve their problems," Papa explained.

"Yeah, people are amazing," Anders said.

"They really are," Mama agreed. "And you just wait, Anders. People are going to invent even more amazing things in your lifetime. It's such an exciting time to be alive."

23. Pretend and Extinct

Now Mama and Anders were in the car on their way to the California Science Center.

"Mama," Anders said, looking out the window, "are dragons scary?"

"Well," Mama said, "are dragons real or pretend?"

"Pretend," Anders answered.

"So, what do you think? Should I be afraid of something that's just pretend?" Mama asked.

"No," Anders said.

"That's what I think too," Mama said. "But we can *pretend* we are afraid of dragons if we want. Do you want to pretend you are afraid of dragons?"

"No," Anders said. He looked out the window for another minute. "If I see a pretend dragon, do you see it too?"

"What do you think?" Mama asked.

"No," Anders answered.

"You're right," Mama said. "When you see a pretend dragon, that's called imagining. Seeing is with your eyes. Imagining is with your mind. I can imagine a dragon too, but it won't be the same one you are imagining. Are you imagining a dragon right now?"

"Yeah," Anders said.

Mama and Anders discussed the difference between real and imagined things frequently. Mama noticed that the better Anders understood the difference between reality and fantasy, the more confident he seemed to be. She had also noticed that he was not afraid of pretend things the way many young children were. Anders had never in his life worried about monsters, not even at bedtime.

Soon Mama and Anders were in the Science Center. They were at the space shuttle exhibit.

The room itself was huge and impressive to Anders. But as soon as he saw the space shuttle, he could not take his eyes off it. It was black and white. It looked official and powerful. Anders walked around it, inspecting it closely. It was a long walk! It took hundreds of steps to walk around the entire thing.

A boy in a Spider-Man costume was also in the room looking at the space shuttle.

"Mama, is Spider-Man pretend or extinct?" Anders asked Mama later, when they were driving home. Anders had never seen a Spider-Man movie or cartoon, but somehow, he knew who Spider-Man was.

"Pretend," Mama said. "Extinct means it existed, and then it died. Pretend means it never existed except in someone's imagination."

"So, Batman is pretend?" Anders asked.

"Correct," Mama said.

"And Great-Grandpa Bud is extinct?" Anders asked.

"Yes," Mama said. "Though extinct means a group of things. Great-Grandpa Bud is one thing, so we say that he died. If all the humans on the planet died, then humans would be extinct. But one human is dead, not extinct."

"Mama," Anders said thoughtfully, "can we pretend we are astronauts?"

"Of course. Would you like to be the pilot?" Mama asked.

"Yes," Anders said. "Okay, we have to press all these buttons! And fly really far!"

"Where are we flying to, Sir?" Mama asked.

"We have to fly by these asteroids. Oh no, they might hit our ship!" Anders said.

"Let's turn the ship so it doesn't hit the asteroids!" Mama said.

"Oh, good we got past the asteroids!" Anders said. "Now I can see penis up ahead! Let's go there! Penis is my favorite planet!"

24. Trying Kumon Again

There was an excellent math program offered in Los Angeles called Kumon. Mama took Anders there right after he turned three, but he didn't like it. Now Anders was six months older, so it was time to try again.

"Anders, you're three and half. Do you think you are ready to learn about numbers?" Mama asked.

"Yes," Anders said. "I want to know what a lowercase two looks like!"

Mama drove Anders to the nearest Kumon. It was a large, no-frills room located in a nearby shopping center. The room was divided into two areas: a classroom area with child-sized tables and chairs where children did their work and a small waiting area with adult-sized chairs where parents waited for their children. There was a sign dividing the two areas.

"This sign says I can't go any further," Mama explained to Anders. "It says only children can enter the classroom area. I will wait here for you."

"Okay," Anders said excitedly, not fazed at all by the thought of leaving his mom behind or entering a classroom full of kids he didn't know. He kissed

Mama goodbye, walked straight into the classroom area, and took a seat in a small chair where a young man had motioned for him to sit.

The man sat down opposite Anders. On the small table between them was a packet of Kumon work. The packet had ten pages. On the front page was a picture of a single apple.

"One," the man said, pointing to the apple. "Can you do that?" he asked.

Anders pointed to the apple and said, "One."

"Good!" the man said.

He turned the page. There was a picture of two cats. "One, two," he said, pointing to each of the cats while he counted.

Anders again mimicked him.

"One, two," Anders said.

The man turned the page. They counted to three and then four. Anders thought this was great fun. He finished the first packet of ten pages quickly.

"Do you want to do more?" the man asked.

"More!" Anders said excitedly.

The man got the next ten-page packet, and they worked through it just as quickly.

"You have done two whole packets of work now Anders, do you want—" the man started to ask.

"More!" Anders interrupted him.

The man got a stack of packets. He stopped asking if Anders wanted to keep going. He just kept going.

After Anders had worked at counting with the man for thirty minutes, the man said, "All right, we are all done. You did eighty pages. You did amazing!"

Anders was horrified. He wasn't all done.

"No, not done," Anders said.

"We did thirty minutes," the man said. "You did *eighty* pages. It's time for you to go home now. Don't you want to go home?"

"No," Anders said. "I want to count more!"

The man thought about this for a second. "That's fine with me if it's fine with your mom. Let me go ask," he said.

The man disappeared for a minute. He found Mama reading in the waiting area and asked her if Anders could keep working, as he did not want to leave yet.

"Sure," Mama said. "We have no other plans today. He can stay as long as he wants."

Anders and the man went back to work. Anders counted and counted. The numbers kept getting bigger and bigger. He moved from counting objects to reading numbers. He was so excited! Numbers were so interesting! As the numbers got bigger, he loved them even more. He couldn't wait to get to one hundred.

Anders wasn't done until he had worked for an hour and half and had done almost two hundred pages of Kumon work. The owner of the center, an elegant Japanese woman named Mrs. Suji, brought Anders out to Mama. She was laughing and laughing.

"He loves it," she said. "He didn't want to go home! But he's so tired. He needs to stop now."

Mama smiled. Anders looked exhausted but happy. Mrs. Suji showed Mama Anders's homework, work that Mama was expected to do with him every day.

"It should never take longer than twenty minutes," she said. "We don't want him to burn himself out."

Mrs. Suji put Anders's homework inside a little blue canvas pouch which she handed to Anders.

"This is your very own bag," she said. "Take good care of it. Don't lose it."

Anders hugged the pouch to his chest.

"See you on Friday," Mrs. Suji said.

"See you Friday!" Anders said. He took Mama's hand, and they walked to the car.

"So… I guess you like this class now?" Mama asked.

"I LOVE this class," Anders said. "I'm going to learn to count to a hundred!"

"That's exciting," Mama said. "There are so many things you will be able to understand too, like money. You have to know about numbers to know about money."

"I LOVE money!" said Anders.

They reached the car. Anders, in his tired and excited state, did not open his car door as he normally did. He walked right into it—*whap!*

25. Intimidation

Now Nathan, the contractor, was at the house. Nathan was a short, well-dressed man with a brusque personality and a thick Israeli accent. He did a quick walkthrough of the kitchen.

"We are done," he said. "I need the final payment now."

"But… what about finishing touches?" Mama asked.

"There are no finishing touches. We are done," Nathan said.

Mama showed Nathan a half-dozen places on the wall that were not smooth like the rest of the wall, edges around the sink that lacked silicone, corners of the countertop where grout needed to be added, removed, or sanded down, places where the brand new cupboards and drawers needed to be touched up because his workers had chipped them, and a scratch one of his workers had left on the new countertop that needed to be buffed out.

Nathan was horrified.

"This is crazy!" he yelled. "You are being too particular! This is fine! This work is fine! Give me my money! You owe me fifteen thousand dollars! Give it to me!"

Mama froze. She was good at dealing with children who were experiencing strong emotions. With adults, she knew the best approach was the same, but she had no experience. Also, though Mama wanted to use good communication to help Nathan feel heard, she felt scared. Nathan was yelling and stomping his feet in an aggressive way. He was getting too close to her and invading her space. Mama worried he was going to become violent.

Mama walked to the front door and opened it.

"You think the work is fine," Mama said, repeating Nathan's words to him in the hopes that it would calm him. She stepped outside. It was the middle of the workday. The sidewalk was empty, and no cars drove down the street. She still wasn't safe.

"I hear you," Mama said. "You think the work is done, and you want to be paid. You have worked hard, and people should be paid for their work."

Nathan did not calm down at all, but he did follow Mama outside which was a relief. At least he was out of the house.

Nathan put his face as close to Mama's as he could get, and said menacingly, "Give me my money now, or you will hear from my lawyer!"

"I want to pay you," Mama said. "You have done work. You will be paid. I can see you are angry and disappointed—"

"You will regret this!" Nathan screamed.

Then he stormed off.

Mama was shaken. She felt faint with relief that he was gone. Anders came outside.

"We all get mad," Anders said. "But we figure it out and get happy again. Sometimes we get mad. Sometimes we get frustrated. Sometimes we get sad. That's how it goes."

"Yeah," Mama agreed. "Did Nathan's yelling stress you out?"

"No," Anders said. "He'll figure it out."

"Will you give me a hug?" Mama asked. "His yelling stressed me out!"

Anders gave Mama a big hug.

Mama called Papa to complain about how useless her communication skills had been.

"It sounds like Nathan wasn't an emotional person who needed to be heard," Papa said. "He wasn't genuinely upset. He was using aggressive tactics to intimidate you. I deal with people like that in business all the time. He probably thought you were inexperienced in business, and so those tactics would work on you. But they didn't! You crushed it!"

Papa laughed heartily.

Mama didn't know what Nathan's plans were, but her goal was for the kitchen to be finished. The finishing touches needed to happen. She had hired Nathan for a job, and she wanted him to finish it. She didn't know what to do to make that happen, so she called her friend Kathi who was experienced in working with contractors. Kathi knew exactly what Mama should do.

Mama spent the next hour taking pictures of all the areas of work that looked sloppy or unfinished. She took thirty-seven pictures. She posted them on Facebook, Google, and Yelp.

"Here are samples of Nathan's company's work," she wrote in her reviews. Within an hour a man called, claiming to be Nathan's lawyer. He told Mama to take down her reviews, or Nathan would sue her for defamation.

"He would lose the suit if he tried that," Mama said. "I have said nothing negative about Nathan's company in my reviews—I merely posted pictures of his work. If he is proud of the work, and I am just too particular, then he should be fine with the pictures. If he is ashamed of the work and agrees that's not what a finished product should look like, then he should come and fix it."

"If he fixes it, will you take the pictures down?" the man asked.

"Of course," Mama said. "If Nathan does better work, my pictures will no longer be representative of his work."

The man put Mama on hold for a few minutes. Then he told her Nathan would be there the next day to fix all the issues.

Mama didn't want to be alone in the house with Nathan, so Kathi came over. Kathi wasn't just there for moral support though: she took over all the communication with Nathan, relieving Mama of a task that would have caused her a great deal of anxiety.

When the finishing touches were done, Mama inspected it and gave Nathan his final payment. After Nathan had gone Mama thanked Kathi over and over.

"I am so grateful to have you for a friend!" Mama said.

"It was nothing!" Kathi said.

"No," Mama said. "It was everything. You just jumped in and saved the day. I feel so cared for. I will never forget this."

26. Rewriting Your Childhood

Now the kitchen was done, and for the first time in six months Mama and Anders could cook again.

"This kitchen is amazing!" Mama said. "I love our new stove."

"Me too!" Anders said. "It's soooooo beautiful."

"I am so excited to have homecooked food again! What should we make today?" Mama asked, opening the new fridge.

"Liver fritters!" Anders said. Mama got out a pound of chicken livers, an onion, bacon, and a large potato.

"Do you want to practice chopping?" Mama asked.

"Yes, I love chopping," Anders said, pushing his kitchen stool over to the corner where he liked to work.

Mama handed him a small knife.

"Can you show me how to chop safely?" she asked.

Anders held the knife in his right hand with the sharp edge down and his left hand flat across the dull edge.

"Great," Mama said.

Mama peeled the potato and cut it into long strips the size of thin French fries. Then she handed the cutting board to Anders.

"Your job is to make perfect little squares out of these pieces of potato, like this," she said.

Mama cut a few squares.

"It's much harder than it looks to make things the same size. You must control your hand. It will want to be sloppy and make pieces that are bigger or smaller than you want. Your goal is to keep all the pieces the exact same size. If they are the same size, they will cook at the same rate and be done at the same time. Then your dish will be tastier," she explained.

Anders went to work. He carefully chopped each long strip of potato into little squares. Mama watched him for a few minutes. His little squares were as good as she could have done herself.

"Anders, you are doing flawless work," Mama said.

Mama went about slicing the onion and cutting up the livers. She constantly checked on Anders to make sure he was still chopping safely while she floured the liver pieces and heated the frying pans.

When Anders was done cutting up the potato pieces, Mama put them in a large frying pan. Anders moved his stool over to the stove and used a small spatula to stir the potatoes as they cooked. While Anders focused on the potatoes, Mama cooked the bacon, the onion, and the liver fritters.

When the food was done cooking Anders sprinkled salt over the top of each thing. That was his favorite part.

Soon Mama and Anders were sitting down to eat breakfast with Papa.

"I am so happy to not be eating restaurant food or microwave food right now," Mama said.

"Me too," said Anders.

"Me three," said Papa. "This is so good, you guys."

After breakfast Papa, Mama, and Anders went outside. The day was hot already.

The house had a small pool in the backyard, with wide steps at the shallow end. Anders had always loved the pool, even though he could not swim and had to stay on the steps.

Mama did not buy Anders any devices that would make him float, because she had read that such devices gave children an artificial sense of security in the water and were therefore dangerous. They also made children less interested in learning to swim. Anders was perfectly content playing on the steps, so Mama didn't see the point in them anyway.

This summer they had been using the pool every day since May. Anders had been staying on the steps as he had last summer, but unlike last summer, he was hopping back and forth instead of walking.

Two weeks ago, some friends came over. One friend was a seven-year-old boy named Chris. Chris could swim. The whole time he was swimming Anders stood perfectly still on the steps and watched his every move. The stroke Chris used was dog paddle, and it made more sense to Anders than the stroke he had seen Papa use.

Ever since Chris came over, Anders's hops had gotten longer and longer, until he was dog-paddling the way Chris had.

"Anders, do you want to show Papa what you have figured out how to do?" Mama asked.

"Yes!" said Anders. He grabbed the swimming trunks that were hanging on the fence near the pool, drying from the last time they had been used. He quickly changed into them, stood on the edge of the pool just past the steps, and jumped in.

The water swished over his head, but he popped right up and dog-paddled to the steps. Then he got out of the pool, went back to the same spot on the edge of the pool, and jumped in again.

"WHAT?!" Papa said, freaking out. "You figured out how to swim?!"

Anders giggled with glee and kept doing what he was doing—jumping into the pool, dog-paddling a short way to the steps, climbing out, and jumping in again.

"He did this for hours today," Mama said.

"I can't believe he taught himself to swim," Papa said. "I'm speechless. He's only three."

"Yup," Mama said.

"And no pushing from us at all," Papa said.

"Nope," Mama said.

"No being shamed for being scared," Papa said.

"Nope," Mama said.

"Or being viciously thrown in," Papa said.

"Nope," Mama said. "I remember being thrown into a lake against my will by an uncle of mine."

"My dad used to push me into the ocean on a boogie board," Papa said. "I would be screaming 'No!' and crying, and he would just send me off."

"It feels like... with each thing we do better than was done to us, wounds from my childhood heal a little. I didn't realize that about having kids. You get to rewrite your own childhood in a way—you get to fix it. Does it feel that way to you too?"

"It does," Papa said.

He took Mama's hand, and she rested her head on his shoulder.

27. Wish Lists

Mama and Anders were in the car driving home after doing several errands.

"Three one zero, five nine three, four eight seven six[5]," Anders said.

Anders had memorized his mom's phone number when he was two and a half, but he had to practice it, or he would forget it. Every time they drove by a certain big, shiny building near their house, that was the cue for Anders to say Mama's number.

"Excellent!" Mama said. "I can't believe you still know my phone number! That is so great in case you ever get lost."

Anders looked out the window. Normally he was proud and excited that he still remembered his mom's phone number, but right now he seemed sad.

"I want a cookie," he said.

"We already went to the store today, Anders, and I did not buy the ingredients for pumpkin cookies. But the next time we go to the store though, we can get the ingredients and make cookies."

---

[5] This is not my real phone number.

Anders burst into tears. Mama was shocked. Anders did not usually react in such a big way to being denied something as little as a cookie. Mama decided to pull the car over, so she could find out what was wrong.

After stopping the car, Mama turned around in her seat.

"Anders, you seem to really want a cookie right now," she mirrored.

"Yeaaaahhh. I need a cookie!" Anders sobbed.

"Anders, maybe you do need a cookie, but it seems to me like maybe you are needing something else. Sometimes, when we think we want a cookie, what we really want is something to sweeten our lives, like a hug or cuddling or support or compassion. Are you needing any of those things?" Mama asked.

Anders thought about this for a minute. Then he said, "I need support."

"What could I do to support you?" Mama asked.

"Buy me a new dump truck," Anders said.

"Ah," Mama said, "You really liked that dump truck we saw at the store today. You wish I had bought it for you."

"Yeah," Anders said sadly. "I really need a new dump truck."

"We took a picture of it," Mama said. "When we get home, we can add it to your birthday list."

Whenever Mama and Anders were out and about and Anders saw something he wanted to buy, Mama handed him her phone, and he took a picture of it.

Then, when they got home, Mama would upload the picture to her computer and put it in a file she kept on her desktop labeled "Anders's Wish List."

Later, when it was near Anders's birthday, they would sit down and go through the folder, deleting pictures of things he no longer wanted and choosing the things he wanted the most to request for his birthday.

Usually, after Anders took a picture of a toy he wanted, he forgot about it almost immediately, but today, he felt sad about not buying the new dump truck.

"But I want the new dump truck *now*," Anders said.

"Waiting is hard," Mama agreed. "I have an idea. How about I hand you my phone, and you can look at the picture you took?"

"Okay!" Anders said.

Mama handed Anders her phone and he looked at the picture for a few seconds. Then he looked at other pictures, pictures of him swimming, of the new kitchen, of him chopping potatoes, of him and Papa wrestling, and more. He forgot all about the toy he didn't have and enjoyed looking at all the wonderful memories he did have.

28. Minimalists and Hoarders

Last month, on a slow Saturday morning Anders had been cuddling with Papa and Mama.

"Do you have any goals or needs for the day?" Papa had asked Anders.

"I want a rest day when nobody comes over and we stay home the whole day," Anders had said.

"That sounds perfect to me!" Papa had said. "I have a big question for us to think about."

"Oooooh, what is it?" Anders had asked.

"I am feeling disillusioned about owning a house in Los Angeles. I can't build a privacy hedge; I can't build a guest house; I can't replace a window without paying five hundred dollars to ask for permission… I don't feel like I really own this house," Papa had said.

Papa was frustrated because city ordinances prevented him and Mama from making the changes to their house that they wanted to make. Papa and Mama didn't know that most ordinances could be fought with the right lawyer, so they assumed that they would never be able to do with their home what they wanted to. This upset them. In Nicaragua they could do what they wanted with their land. They felt free.

"The real estate market is crazy right now," Papa had said. "Our house is worth a lot more money than we paid for it a year ago, especially considering the new kitchen. I'm thinking that we could sell this place, use the money from the sale to finish building our house in Nicaragua, and still have the down payment in our savings account to buy a house in Los Angeles later if we want to."

"And then live at the farm full-time?" Mama had asked.

"Maybe eight months of the year at the farm and four months of the year traveling?" Papa had suggested. "Right now, we spend as much money on our mortgage as it would cost to spend four months in hotels. Why be in Los Angeles when we could be in other places?"

"Nice hotels?" Mama had asked.

"Like Courtyard Marriotts. Not the fanciest, but certainly decent. And maybe the occasional nicer place," Papa had answered.

Courtyard Marriotts were fine with Mama.

"What about your job?" Mama had asked.

"I can do most of it from the farm if we get internet there," Papa had said. "When I need to, I can fly back for meetings."

"What an interesting idea," Mama had said. "Half farmers and half jetsetters. What do you think Anders? Would you like to live at the farm most of the time and then do traveling to different places and go on lots of adventures?"

"I love it!" Anders had said.

"You won't be sad if we sell this house? You're not too attached to it?" Mama had asked.

"No," Anders had said.

"So instead of one giant city, we can do lots of giant cities," Mama had said. "But probably mainly Los Angeles since your classes are here and our friends are here…."

"Let's take some time to think it over," Papa had said. "It's a big decision. We would probably travel mostly to Los Angeles, but we would also be free to check out other places if we wanted."

Now they had thought it over for a month and, being young and full of energy, they decided to do it. Papa met with a real estate agent named Lynne. She advised them to spend five thousand dollars adding a fresh coat of paint to every room of house.

"Do that, and you will sell this house for twenty thousand dollars more," she said.

So, Mama had every room of the house painted in fresh, beautiful colors. The next time Lynne came over she was blown away.

"I always tell people to do that," she said, "and they never do. This looks amazing!"

In two weeks, the house was sold. Mama and Anders spent all of their time going through stuff. They sold everything they could, donated what they couldn't, and put essential items aside for the storage unit Papa had rented.

"I love getting rid of stuff," Mama said. "I love going through everything and deciding if it is worth keeping. Moving to another country is an excellent exercise in deciding what is essential. Not much is."

"Minimalism is a kind of overconfidence," Mama's Grandma Natalie had told her once. "I grew up in the depression. Many things you think you will never use come in handy during hard times. You should appreciate your stuff more. And save more of it. And you should have more meat on your bones. Your generation would die like flies during a famine. An extra twenty pounds is an extra month of life when there are food shortages."

"Okay, hoarder!" Mama said. "That is interesting food for thought though."

29. Traveling with Young Kids

Now they were at the airport. It was time to board their airplane. Anders loved boarding airplanes! He loved walking down the gangway. It was fun trying to stay balanced at the different angles of the movable corridor. He especially loved the end of the corridor where there was a little inch of space between the gangway and the plane.

The flight attendant said, "Careful!" but he was a careful boy. He always paid close attention when he was stepping over that inch, whether anyone said to or not.

"You are in seat twenty-four," Mama told him. Anders was so excited. He knew how to count and read numbers now, so he was able to find his seat all by himself!

"Twenty-two, twenty-three, twenty-four!" Anders said.

"You are in the seat by the window," Mama said. Anders climbed into his seat. He buckled his seatbelt, and then his eyes were glued out the window. There were so many men out there working on so many different things! There were so many interesting machines to look at!

Soon the plane was in the air. Anders sat in his seat, happily playing with his little animal figurines. When he was done with those, he got out his construction trucks. When he was done with those, he studied the lights above his seat for a while.

Then he met the people sitting around him. Then he ate some snacks. He went to the bathroom a few times just to get up and stretch his legs. Then he fell asleep for a little while. But then, when he woke up, his body started to feel… all penned up.

He wanted to run around! He wanted to climb! He wanted to expend energy. He wanted to do anything but keep sitting and sitting and sitting.

Papa took Anders to the bathroom again. They stopped by the flight attendant area and did some yoga stretches. They managed to stay on their feet for twenty minutes. But eventually, Papa brought an unhappy Anders back to his seat.

"Are you struggling?" Mama asked.

"Yeah," Anders said. "I want to run."

"I know," Mama said. "It's so hard to be stuck on an airplane for five hours. Tell your legs they can run and climb all they want tomorrow at the farm, but today they must sit for the whole day."

Anders looked glumly at his legs.

"Okay, Anders," Mama said. "I see that it is time. You did amazingly. We only have an hour and half left of this flight. So… would you like me to distract you from your discomfort by reading to you?"

"YES," Anders said with a big sigh of relief.

Mama took eight books out of her carry-on. They were new books! They were stories Anders had never heard before! Anders was so excited that he forgot that he wanted to be running around.

Mama read Anders book after book. She read him *Jet Plane: How It Works, Flicka, Ricka, and Dicka Go to Market, Henry and Mudge,* four *Nate the*

Great books, and many chapters from *Where the Red Fern Grows.*

Mama read to Anders for ninety minutes. Then, before Anders even knew it was happening, the plane was landing in Managua, Nicaragua.

Anders got off the plane. It was evening now.

"Can I run now?" Anders asked Mama.

"You can run from here to the baggage claim over there," Mama said. "But after we get our bags, we need to get in the car and drive to the farm. More sitting."

Anders ran to the baggage claim. Mama loved the baggage claim experience in Nicaragua because she did not ever have to touch her bags. As soon as Papa and she arrived in the baggage claim area, a man with a baggage cart, called a porter, approached them and asked them to point out which bags were theirs. The porter took their suitcases off the baggage carousels; he stacked them on the baggage cart; he verified their claim numbers; he took the bags to customs where he put them on conveyer belts that traveled through x-ray machines; then he removed the bags from the conveyer belt and put them back on the baggage cart. Then a second porter took over. He wheeled the cart next to them as they exited the airport.

Outside the airport Papa's friend Kenneth was waiting for them. Despite the late hour, it was hot and humid.

"I remember this place!" Anders said. "This is the place where I can never tell if I am sweating or if I peed my pants!"

30. Workbooks and the Cost of Labor

When Anders woke up the next day, he felt excited. He was at the farm! There was so much to see and do and explore at the farm! He jumped out of bed and went to the rancho.

"Good morning, Nate! Good morning, James!" Anders said.

Nate was sitting at the picnic table waiting for his food. James was making breakfast.

"Good morning, Anders. Happy to be back?" Nate asked.

"So happy!" Anders said.

Anders noticed there was a woman working in the kitchen with James.

"Who's that?" Anders asked.

"That's Dolores," Nate said. "Your mom and dad hired her to help. She does the dishes and the laundry and helps me cook. Why don't you go introduce yourself?"[6]

---

[6] Hiring a full time (48 hours per week) domestic worker in Nicaragua in the year 2016 cost us around $180 per month. (Minimum wage was $140 per month at the time.) I share this because I want my readers to understand just how affordable Nicaragua is.

Anders walked up to Dolores. She was a short, older, Nicaraguan woman with curly black hair and a wide smile. She giggled when Anders shook her hand. He introduced himself in Spanish, and she introduced herself as well, adding that he was precious and had beautiful manners.

"May I have tortillas and eggs for breakfast?" Anders asked James.

Anders had never asked for tortillas and eggs in Los Angeles, but here at the farm he remembered that he liked to have tortillas and eggs for breakfast.

Mama joined Anders in the rancho. Brava, the farm dog, came over wagging her tail. She was so happy to see Anders.

James brought Mama and Anders their breakfasts.

"Mama, how do you say *gracias* in Spanish?" Anders asked.

"*Gracias* is in Spanish, Anders," Mama said. "It means *thank you* in English."

"Oh, gracias for breakfast James," Anders said.

"Yes, thank you, James," Mama said.

Mama shooed a wasp away from her food.

"When we were camping at our house in Los Angeles, I never appreciated how bug free it was," she said. "There are so many wasps in here."

"Yeah, they have nests all over the rancho," James said.

"What?! Where?" Mama asked.

"See that pile of mud on the ceiling over there?" James asked. "That's one kind of wasp nest."

"That's so funny. It looks like someone threw a mud pie at the ceiling, and it stuck," Mama said, going over to examine it. "I had no idea that was a wasp nest."

Sure enough, there were wasps flying in and out of what looked like a mud pie. Mama noticed that there were many mud pies on the ceiling of the rancho. She counted five in all.

"Why don't you guys remove them?" Mama asked.

"They don't really bother us. But if they bother you, I can take them down," Nate said.

"I would love that," Mama said. "Thank you."

"Ok," Nate said, "I'll take them down after breakfast."

Soon the workers arrived. It was the same group of men that had been working on the well the last time Mama and Anders were at the farm. They had been working on the well six days a week the entire time the family had been gone. With them came Erick, the carpenter. Anders greeted all of these old friends. He was so happy to see them again.

In the afternoon. Yesnir, Jesslyn, Moisés, and Ramón came over to play. Anders had brought a whole suitcase of toys that they had never seen before from Los Angeles.

"Look what we brought!" Anders said, excitedly showing them his collection of wooden trains and train tracks. The kids loved the trains and immediately started building a long set of train tracks.

Then Anders got out a stack of workbooks.

"Mama brought workbooks for everyone!" he exclaimed.

The kids were even more excited about the workbooks than they had been about the trains. Anders handed Jesslyn a Kumon maze workbook.

"It's the same as mine, see?" he showed her.

Anders gave Yesnir, Moisés, and Ramón each a math workbook and a much harder maze workbook. For the next hour the kids sat at a table in the rancho and worked on the workbooks. Jesslyn liked her workbook so much that when the boys left to play with the trains, she stayed at the table working on her workbook. Two hours later when it was time to go home, she cried. She wanted to keep working on her workbook.

"You can take it home with you," Mama told her.

Jesslyn was elated. Mama looked through Jesslyn's workbook to see if she was doing a good job. Not only was her work neat and orderly, but she had done almost the entire book.

Anders was happy to be back at the farm. There was so much to do! And so many people to see!

"Anders," Mama said. "Something just happened that I think you would enjoy hearing about. I went to the bathroom. And there was this little dark speck on the toilet seat, so I was super annoyed that someone had been sloppy. But when I went to clean it up, it flew away. It was a mosquito. Just chilling on the toilet seat. Waiting for some butt to sit down. If I hadn't noticed it, it would have bitten me right on my butt."

Anders howled with laughter.

"It would have bitten you on your butt a hundred times!" Anders said. "And then you would have walked around scratching your butt all day!

31. Wasps

Mama noticed that the keyhole on the doorknob to the bedroom was filled with mud.

"Anders, did you get mud in our keyhole?" she asked.

"No, it wasn't me," Anders said.

Mama did not think Anders was lying, but he could be careless.

"Maybe your hands were dirty, and it happened by accident?" she asked.

But that didn't make sense either. If Anders's hands had been dirty, the entire doorknob would have been dirty. And it wasn't. It was just the keyhole, as if someone were specifically filling the keyhole with mud as a prank.

"No," Anders said. "My hands are clean. Look!"

He showed Mama his hands. Mama got a spray bottle full of water and cleaned out the keyhole. She tried her key to make sure it would work, and it did.

The next day, Mama found the keyhole filled with mud again.

"Okay, who is playing a prank on me?" Mama wondered. "Is it one of the kids who visit? Is it just part of life in the jungle? Maybe the wind fills all the keyholes with dirt every day."

Mama went to inspect the doorknobs of the other rooms. None of them had keyholes filled with mud like hers, so that theory must be incorrect.

Mama decided one of the kids was playing a prank on her. That day, when Yesnir, Jesslyn, Moisés, and Ramón came over, Mama asked them if they were filling her doorknob with mud. They insisted that they weren't and would never do such a thing.

Then Mama asked Nate and James if they were playing a prank on her. They thought she was crazy for even asking them.

A few days later, when Mama was sitting on the patio talking to Nate, they saw a small, agile jungle wasp fly right into the keyhole on the doorknob to Mama's room. They watched it for a minute. It looked like it was working on something in there. Then it flew away. A few moments later, it returned.

Mama smiled.

"Of course. A wasp," she said to Nate. "The jungle was playing a prank on me."

"Ha!" Nate said. "The jungle plays lots of pranks."

32. Cheap Things Are Costly

Mama was in the bedroom studying. Anders came in. He took one of Papa's special tools from one of the suitcases and started to walk outside with it.

"Anders," Mama said, "that belongs to Papa, and he does not want it to get dirty."

Anders thought about this for a moment.

"Can I have two more chances?" he inquired.

Mama smiled.

"No," she said. "No more chances. You were about to do something wrong—you were taking someone else's thing without asking. I stopped you. You should not continue to try and do the wrong thing. You should put it back and thank me for stopping you," she said.

Anders looked at Mama for a moment, considering what she had said. Then he sighed.

"Thank you, Mama," he said, returning the tool to the suitcase. "I put it back."

"I'm so proud of you," Mama said. "We all make bad choices sometimes, and if we're lucky someone stops us before we cause any trouble. If I am ever making a bad choice, will you make sure to stop me?"

"Yes," Anders said. "What bad choices will you make?"

"I forget to brush my teeth in the morning sometimes. After breakfast, I should go straight to the bathroom. If you see me skipping the bathroom and going to my room, you can stop me," Mama said.

"Okay," Anders said enthusiastically. "I will help you, Mama."

Papa came into the bedroom.

"I need to talk to you guys," Papa said. "Remember how we bought the cheapest air conditioner in existence, and it didn't work at all, so it was a total waste of two hundred and fifty dollars?" he asked.

"I remember," Mama said.

"Remember how you said it would be the same with the well?" Papa asked.

"Yes," Mama said.

Papa looked sadly at Mama and Anders.

"After nine months of digging we have a hand-dug well that is seventy-six feet deep. It produces only a hundred gallons of water a day. A hundred gallons of water is enough for one person to bathe, wash dishes, cook, and do laundry. It is not enough for a family, and it is nowhere near enough for a farm…. I came to tell you guys that the water witch was wrong. It is time to hire people with a special machine that can dig down to five hundred feet, if necessary," he said.

"Oh my gosh! We can finally move on!" Mama said happily, throwing her arms around Papa. "I'm so sorry you didn't get what you wanted though."

"I'm sorry too, Papa," Anders said. "Is there anything I can do to help you feel better?"

"How about a wrestling match?" Papa asked. "Wrestling always puts me in a good mood."

"What?!" Anders exclaimed. "Wrestling always puts me in a good mood too!"

Papa grabbed Anders and threw him over his shoulder. Then he carried him to the bed and dropped him onto the bed.

Anders laughed with delight. Papa made a big show of being about to jump on top of Anders and tackle him. Anders quickly rolled several times to the side of the bed.

"I'm going to pound you into a pulp!" Papa said.

Papa sprang to where Anders had been just moments before.

"What?!" Papa said in mock surprise. "Where did you go!? You are too fast!"

Anders giggled. Papa was on all fours looking for Anders. He looked the wrong way. This gave Anders time to climb onto Papa's back.

"You're going down!" Anders said.

33. Taking Advantage of Foreigners

Papa went to Juigalpa for a meeting with a well-digging company. Mama and Anders wanted to get off the farm for a day, so they tagged along. Juigalpa was a small city that was a forty-minute drive from the farm. The meeting was at a restaurant.

Papa, Mama, and Anders arrived first. The well diggers arrived fifteen minutes later. There were four of them. One, Antonio, was the boss. He was older than the rest and quite fat. His clothes had Tommy Hilfiger and Ralph Lauren labels.

Another of the men was the boss's son. He was also quite fat and dressed in designer labels like his father.

The two other men looked like laborers. They were fit, muscular, and though they looked put-together, their clothes had no labels on them.

Papa talked to the men for an hour. They showed him pictures and videos of their well-digging machine. The men didn't speak English, so when the conversation got far enough along that Papa wanted to ask about technical things he didn't know enough Spanish to discuss, Papa called Ken, and Ken translated. Finally, Papa said their machine would do the job, and he and Antonio struck a deal.

"Are they going to come to the farm?" Anders asked Papa when the meeting was over.

"Yup," Papa said. "With a special truck. You are going to love it."

Papa planned to spend a week getting everything at the farm ready for the well diggers. A road had to be made from the driveway to the digging site. Antonio had recommended digging in the creek bed. He said that was the place they would be most likely to hit water.

Carving a road through the wilderness to the creek bed was not an easy task. There were trees that had to be chopped down. There was endless brush to clear. Papa thought it would take a week, but Nate, who had been living at the farm for two years now, had become experienced with a machete and strong from manual labor. He cleared the path in two days. Cutting down trees always made Nate sad, especially since the trees that had to be cut down were young rainforest trees, but it had to be done.

Now the well-digging day was here. Everyone was excited, but no one was more excited than Anders. Antonio and his workers arrived right after breakfast. They drove two huge trucks. The trucks lumbered up the driveway, then turned down the new road Nate had cleared for them. When they were about thirty feet from the creek, they stopped.

Antonio said the trucks could not continue because the road was too rough, so they would dig there.

"This is not the digging spot," Papa said.

"Eh, we're close enough. Let's just dig here," Antonio said.

Six laborers jumped out of the truck and started digging in preparation for the drill.

"No," Papa said. "I need to hit water the first time we drill. And over there is the spot you advised us to drill. If you don't want to drill there, I don't have any work for you today."

Antonio pressured Papa to let him drill where he wanted, but Papa stood firm. It was quite tense for a while, but eventually Antonio agreed to dig in the spot he had recommended if the last thirty feet of road were made smoother.

Papa, Nate, Anders, Erick, Erick's brother Herman (who had come to help for the day), and the six laborers who came with Antonio, got pickaxes, crowbars, and shovels and worked as fast as they could, leveling the last thirty feet of road. Antonio and his son did not help. They smoked cigarettes and watched the other men work.

After an hour, the last thirty feet of road was level enough. Antonio drove the drill truck to the digging spot. The drill was set up. Then the machine started going. It made a lot of noise and spewed dust while it dug through layer upon layer of rock

By noon the machine was hitting some water, and mud started to squirt out around the drill. Anders sat with the workers and watched the drill. Several times Anders tried to get closer to the drill to learn more about it, but various men stopped him because it was not safe.

When Anders became hungry, he walked to the rancho. There, he found out that it was lunch time, but he was too excited to sit down for lunch, so he gulped down a glass of milk and headed back to the digging site.

Antonio came to the rancho to talk to Mama.

"Do you have lunch for us?" he asked.

"I had no idea you were expecting lunch," Mama said.

"Yeah, you are supposed to give us lunch," he said.[7] "That is the custom here."

"Okay," Mama said. "It will take a little bit, but I will get you something!"

James was asleep in his room. Dolores usually just cleaned and did not do any cooking, but she knew exactly what to do in this situation. She made a large pitcher of juice and sent it to the guys immediately.

---

[7] Papa and Mama did not owe Antonio and his workers lunch. Antonio was taking advantage of them because they were foreigners and he assumed, rightly, that he could trick them into giving him and his workers a free lunch.

They drank the entire pitcher while they waited for their lunch. Soon, Dolores had plates of beans, rice, fried plantains, and scrambled eggs ready. Mama and Dolores carried the plates of food to the workers. They were happy to get the food.

Now it was the afternoon, and the machine was still going. It was getting muddier and muddier at the site. Yesnir came over and joined Anders in watching the drill. After a while, Yesnir convinced Anders to take a short swimming break. The mud pile grew exponentially while they were gone. When they got back it was the biggest pile of mud Anders had ever seen.

"Papa, can I get really, really dirty?" Anders asked.

"Have at it, Anders. Getting to play in giant piles of mud is one of the best parts about being a farm boy," Papa said happily.

Anders climbed gingerly into the mud pile. He took off his boots so it could squish between his toes. He hopped around in it like a frog. He squeezed it in his hands. He made piles of it. It was thick, smeary, sticky mud, not watery at all. It got all over his whole body. He had never been happier.

"I have always wanted a mud pile like this!" he yelled to Papa. "I dreamed of mud like this!"

Papa nodded.

"I'm pretty sure I dreamed of mud like this when I was a kid too," he said.

Now it was dusk. The drill had dug one hundred and ninety feet down and had finally hit water—lots of water! But they weren't quite done. The drill dug for another hour. It was pitch black out when the drill finally stopped. The well was two hundred feet deep. The men put pipes in, first big ones, then medium-sized ones, then little ones.

Papa wrapped a very muddy Anders in a towel and held him while helping direct the trucks safely down the driveway. By the time they were leaving, it was pitch black except for the headlights of the trucks and the flashlights held by Papa and Nate.

When the trucks were safely on the highway, Papa brought Anders into the rancho. Anders was so covered in mud that Mama pretended she didn't recognize him.

"Oh my gosh, a wild animal!" she said.

Papa handed the "wild animal" to Mama, and she carried him to the shower. It took a long time to get all the mud off. Anders kept asking Mama if his face was clean, and Mama kept saying, "No, not yet!"

Finally, Anders was all clean, and Mama said, "Wait, you're not a wild animal, you're a little boy!"

Anders giggled. "I'm your little boy!" he said.

"What was the best part of your day?" Mama inquired.

"My whole day was the best part of my day!"
Anders said.

34. How to Move Water

A few days later, Papa and Mama stood on the patio watching Anders take his nightly bath in a five-gallon bucket of water.

"Now we have a well," Papa told Mama. "We need to build a pump house as soon as possible to guard the pump, so it cannot be stolen. Then we need to get water tanks up on top of the mountain somehow to create water pressure. And then we will need to put in a bunch of pipes to bring the water from the well to the water tanks on the mountain and from the water tanks on the mountain to the kitchen sink in the rancho and the shower and the bathroom sink. We will need pipes to bring water to the farm, too."

"Wow," Mama said. "So, we are nowhere near done solving the water problem yet."

"No," Papa said. "It's going to take the rest of the year to get everything in place. Then it will have been two years since the first time you and Anders visited the farm and two and a half years for me. For two and a half years, we didn't have enough water for Anders to play in as often as he wanted, or for you to shower or to keep any plants alive during the dry season or to keep animals at the farm. But by January, when I have it all set up, we will be 'water rich.'"

"Will we be able to drink the water?" Mama asked.

"The water needs to be tested and filtered before we can drink it," Papa said.

"Buying undeveloped land is so insane. My whole life I have just turned-on faucets and expected water to come out," Mama said. "I had no concept whatsoever of the amount of effort it takes to make water flow from one place to another. It's awesome to learn these things."

"But a little overwhelming?" Papa asked with a smile.

"Yeah… a little like, 'What have we gotten ourselves into?'" Mama said.

"Yup," Papa said. "I'm exhausted. I'll see you in bed."

Papa headed to the bedroom. Mama turned to Anders.

"Anders, Papa and I are super tired. Are you ready to get out of the bucket?" she asked.

"No," Anders said.

Mama thought for a minute. She remembered that often three-year-olds will change their mind if you use the magic word—surprise.

"What if I pretend like I think you are not going to get out, and I head to bed, and then you sneak out of the bucket and race to the room and get there before me and *surprise* me?" Mama asked.

"Okay!" Anders said, excited. He loved surprises.

"All right, well, I'm going to bed now. Good night, my love," Mama said, smiling at Anders.

Mama turned and walked away slowly looking to the left and then to the right. She paused on the patio outside the door and looked up at the sky.

Anders got out of his bucket as quietly as he could. He grabbed the towel Mama had left for him and scurried up the steps to the patio, giggling the whole time. He opened the door to the bedroom and snuck inside.

A moment later Mama opened the door.

"Surprise!" Anders said.

"What?!" Mama said, her eyes wide. "What just happened! You can't be in here right now! You're outside in your bucket! How did you get in here?"

Anders giggled and giggled.

35. Jungle Wisdom

Now Papa was back in Los Angeles. At first he stayed in a hotel, but without his family to be with in the evening, Papa stopped seeing the point in leaving work. He worked twelve to sixteen hours a day, slept on the couch in his office, and only left work for meetings or to bathe at a nearby gym.

Mama and Anders missed Papa. They had been at the farm without him for over a month. Now, Nate's mom, Becca, was visiting. She had never been to Nicaragua before and was enjoying the farm, but she wanted to see more of the country. Mama and Anders decided to take her Selva Negra, the coffee plantation and eco resort they had enjoyed so much when they had visited the year before. The decided to bring Nate, Yesnir, and Moisés as well.

They all piled into the car. Moisés and Yesnir had never been to the mountains in the north of Nicaragua before and were excited to go on this adventure.

For the first hour of the drive, the boys bounced around in the back of the car, making jokes and laughing. For the next hour they were quieter and looked out the windows a great deal.

Then Moisés asked, "How much longer?"

"We are about halfway there," Mama said.

Anders fell asleep. Mama recommended that the boys do the same thing. They looked out the windows a while longer, and then they did as Mama had advised.

When they arrived, the boys were shocked at how cold it was. In the area of Nicaragua where they lived, Chontales, the coldest it *ever* got was seventy degrees. Selva Negra was seventy degrees at noon. In the morning and evening the temperatures there were in the sixties.

Anders was excited to see Selva Negra again. He showed the boys around the main lodge. On the second floor, there was a small museum that told the history of Selva Negra. There were pictures of the first German immigrants that came there in the late nineteenth century. Beneath glass cases lay the tools they used to build their little Bavarian-style cabins and farm the land. All of it was interesting to the boys.

When Mama was checking in, she noticed a sign advertising night tours of the jungle. She asked the boys if that was something they would like to do.

"Yes!" they all said.

They brought their bags to their rooms. They walked around the lake. The kids played on the playground for a while. Then it was dinner time. The group sat at a table on a large patio near a beautiful, manmade lake.

Mama ordered a plate of German sausages. Nate ordered a schnitzel. Anders ordered a cheese and charcuterie plate. Becca ordered a soup and a salad. Mama asked Yesnir and Moisés if they wanted a typical Nicaraguan meal. They didn't. They wanted to try something new. After a short discussion about the options, they both ordered steaks.

Mama, Anders, Nate, and Becca were pleased with their meals. Yesnir and Moisés were elated. They said steak was the best thing they had ever tasted.

Now it was time to meet José, their guide for the night tour, in the lobby. The boys found him easily. He was a lively, engaging man who spoke both English and Spanish. He led the group to a path leading into the jungle.

"Before we go into the jungle, while we are still here at the edge, can anyone find me a cricket?" he asked in Spanish.

The boys immediately started hunting around and pointed out several crickets on leaves on the side of the path.

"Good!" José said. "You found out that there are many crickets in the jungle."

Moisés reached out as if he were going to catch the cricket.

"Ah-ah-ah, don't get too close," José said. "Somewhere nearby there is a frog that wants to eat that cricket. Can you find the frog?"

The boys began a new hunt for a frog. It took them a minute or two, but they soon spotted a large frog about two feet away from the cricket they had found.

"Good!" José said. "I'm serious! Excellent work! Ah-ah-ah don't get too close," he said as again Moisés appeared as if he wanted to catch the frog.

"Somewhere near that frog is a snake that wants to eat that frog. Can you find the snake for me?" José asked.

Now José had the boys' attention. Moisés was no longer interested in getting close to the frog. Instead, he and Yesnir huddled together in the very center of the path. They wanted to be as far from the jungle as they could. Anders grabbed Mama's hand. They too moved to the center of the path.

No one wanted to help José find the snake, so he looked around for a minute or two and found one. It wasn't a particularly dangerous snake, but everyone got the message.

José said, "Where you see a cricket, there is a frog. Where there is a frog, there is a snake. This is why we stay in the middle of the path on this tour, and we do not touch the leaves… and we do not go near the crickets."

For the rest of the tour the boys stayed in the middle of the path, and so did Mama, Becca, and Nate. The tour was fun. José pointed out many small animals, many kinds of birds, and many different species of giant trees. The group's favorite thing of the night was a huge *mata-árbol*.

"This is a special tree," José told the group. "Because… it is not really a tree."

"What?!" Anders exclaimed. "That is a tree."

"It looks just like a tree," Mama said, confused.

José got close to the ground near one of the roots and shined his large flashlight into the tree.

"See in there?" he asked. "There was a tree here once, a big, old tree. But then a special vine called a *mata-árbol* began to surround the tree. It probably took a hundred years, the vine feeding off the tree and slowly, slowly covering it. Today, you can no longer see the tree. What you see on the outside here, that looks like a tree, is actually… a vine. That is why the vine is called a *mata-árbol*. It means *tree-killer*."

"We have one of these at the farm," Nate told everyone.

"You're joking!" Mama said.

"No, I'm not. It looks just like this. I'll show it to you when we get back," Nate said.

"Are you kidding us?" Anders asked.

"No," Nate said. "I'm totally serious."

He was. One of the biggest trees at the farm, a tree that Papa, Mama, and Anders had always admired, did in fact turn out to be a *mata-árbol*.

36. Heroic Men

After three nights at Selva Negra, it was time to go home. Anders, Yesnir, Moisés, and Becca piled into the back of the car. Nate, who was quite tall, sat in the front passenger seat, and Mama drove.

The boys talked about everything they had done at Selva Negra and looked out the windows. After they had been in the car for about two hours, a large, nice, white pick-up truck passed them. As it was passing the driver rolled down his window and gave Mama a thumbs-down sign.

"What does that mean?" Mama asked Moisés and Yesnir.

"I don't know," said Yesnir.

"It means you're slower than he is, and you're lame!" said Moisés.

Mama didn't think that was it. The man hadn't had a mean look on his face; he had had a helpful look. Mama thought maybe the thumbs-down sign meant there were police ahead, and she should drive carefully. Or maybe it meant she should go slower while he was passing her.

In ten minutes, Mama found out what the thumbs-down sign really meant. It meant Mama had a flat tire. Mama pulled over to the side of the highway.

It was late afternoon, so the temperature was just hot, not scorching. They had water in the car, so no one was going to get heat stroke or become dehydrated. Luckily, the flat tire had happened in an area with cellphone service, so Mama was able to call Papa and alert him to the situation. Even more luck was with them because Becca knew what to do to change a tire. She quickly found the jack and a spare tire under a rug in the back of the car.

Becca set about telling Nate how to jack up the car. Because it was the first time Nate had ever done this, it took quite a long time for him to get the jack going—and when he finally managed to make the jack lift the car, he learned the hard way that the jack was not at the right angle: the car fell off the jack.

Nate set about trying again, and again the car fell off the jack.

"Don't worry guys. I'll figure it out," Nate said. He and Becca examined the jack, trying to figure out what they were doing wrong. They set up the jack a third and a fourth time, but both times the car fell off the jack as soon as they tried to lift it up.

The group had been at the side of the road for about forty-five minutes when a huge truck full of cows pulled over right behind them. A large, muscular, Nicaraguan man got out. He asked if they needed help.

"Yes, I am having trouble jacking up the car, so I can change our flat tire," Nate said in Spanish.

"Ah," the man said. He went to his truck and got a tire hammer. Then he took the jack from Nate and within less than a minute, he had the car jacked up off the ground. With his hammer he hit the flat tire at an angle so exact that the tire came right off. In less than five minutes he had the spare tire on the car.

Nate and Becca thanked the man profusely. Mama told him that he was their hero. He nodded at them and smiled. Then he hopped back into his truck and drove away.

"I can't believe what just happened," Becca said. "That was so fast."

The stranger's performance was so impressive that for the rest of the drive—and for years afterward—everyone said that the stranger had held the car up with one hand and changed the tire with his other hand. That's how effortless he had made it look.

"I was feeling so manly and useful," Nate said. "And then this guy shows up. By the time he leaves, I feel like a teeny, tiny, little bug!"

37. Beauty Is Objective

Nicaragua is near the equator, so sunsets are short, and darkness falls quickly. There is little seasonal change in the time that darkness falls. Near the summer solstice it is dark by 7:00 p.m., and near the winter solstice it is dark by 6:15 p.m.

Now it was October. It was 7:00 p.m., so it wasn't just dark out, it was pitch black, except for a single light bulb that hung from the ceiling of the rancho. It was the night before Anders's fourth birthday. Anders, Papa, Mama, James, and Nate were in the rancho hanging out. Anders sat on Papa's lap.

"When you were a baby, Anders, we didn't even own this property yet. When you were one year old, I was buying this property. When you were two years old, I spent my first night here. There were no buildings then except for the rancho, and there was no electricity yet." Papa said.

"So, it was very dark," Anders said.

"Yes," Papa said. "So dark I couldn't see my hand in front of my face."

"Were you scared?" Mama asked.

"Ummm, yes," Papa answered laughing. Then he told a story:

"My first night here, it was just me and Nate in this rancho. We slept in cots, and we had to go to bed as soon as it got dark because there was no electricity yet.

The first night I was here, Nate fell right to sleep. He was out cold the minute he lay down. It took me a long time to go to sleep. I felt so exposed. I was in a three-sided building. In a tent when you are camping, at least you have tent walls all around you. We didn't even have that.

So, I finally got to sleep. And then, a couple hours into the night, there was this rustling sound, like a wild animal. I woke up. I was terrified.

"What am I doing?" I thought. "I am sleeping totally exposed to nature!"

I whispered to Nate.

I said, "Nate there's an animal!" Nate didn't move. The animal made this low, growling noise.

So, I said it louder, "Nate, there's an animal!" Nate didn't even flinch. I was freaking out. I started thinking he was dead.

So, I yelled really loudly, "NATE, THERE'S AN ANIMAL!!!"

Nate finally woke up and was like, "Huh?" Then he said, "Oh, it's probably just a dog in the trash bin over there," and he went back to sleep.

And I was like, "Okay. I'm just supposed to sleep while wild dogs growl ten feet from me?"

It took me a long time to get back to sleep. And then, when I was finally asleep again, I heard this *de du de du de du*

sound of a large animal. I opened my eyes.
Now the moon was out, so I could see a
little bit. And what I saw was a *huge* dark
shape running by. I jumped out of my skin
and screamed!"

Papa was laughing so hard while telling this
story that tears came out of his eyes.

"What happened? What happened?" Anders
asked. Papa continued his story:

"Nate woke up when I screamed
and said, "It's just a horse! It's just a
horse! She does that."

And then he went right back to
sleep. Apparently, our neighbor's horse
escaped and went for night runs fairly
often.

Anyway, that was my first night
here. It was scary. But truly awesome
too."

Anders laughed.

"It was just a horse!" he said.

"Yeah," Papa said. "When we woke up in the
morning, I did not feel like I had slept at all. But we
got up, made some noodles on our little camping
stove, and ate them with hot sauce and cans of tuna.
Then we spent the day literally crawling through the

jungle on our hands and knees. We were exploring and imagining where we would build things. It's crazy thinking we are about to build the main building, just two years later."

"Are we sure we want to build it? And not start over?" Mama asked.

Mama had been reading architecture books by Christopher Alexander. He wrote about objective beauty in architecture. He wrote that beauty begat beauty and ugliness begat ugliness. He wrote that if a building was ugly, it was better to demolish it and start over than to try to save it.

The first buildings that Papa had had built at the farm were ugly. Papa hadn't done much more to design those buildings than draw a rectangular shape on a piece of paper. He let Max, the contractor, make most of the design decisions, like how tall and wide the doorways would be and the shapes of the windows. Beauty, Mama had learned, was all in the ratios. Rectangles with a 3:1 ratio were beautiful. Rectangles with a 2:1 ratio were not. Beauty mirrored the rules nature followed. Ugliness didn't follow the rules nature followed.

The building Mama had designed, the building that would become the main building at the farm, started with the ugly rectangle Max had built. Mama added two new wings to it, turning the overall shape of the building into a U. She put a courtyard in the middle with a fountain. To create beauty, the Ushaped building must be symmetrical. The other leg of the U would be an exact replica of the rectangle already built. This meant that Mama had to stick with the ugly dimensions of the rooms and the door and the even uglier, almost-square, dimensions of the windows.

The drawing Mama made of the new building had taken months and many iterations, but it did look nice on paper—perhaps even beautiful. Even though Christopher Alexander did not recommend trying to save an ugly building, Papa thought Mama had.

"I want to build the new building!" said Anders. "It's beautiful."

"If Anders thinks it's beautiful, then I think we should go for it," Papa said. "Anders has a good eye for these things."

"True. It will never be as beautiful as it could have been. But I think it will be beautiful enough to make us happy," Mama said.

"Even with its flaws, it will still be more beautiful than anything else being built today," Papa added.

"That's true," Mama said.

"People build ugly buildings on purpose nowadays," Nate said. "Beautiful buildings are elitist."

"It's also almost impossible because of the building codes. The building codes almost require buildings to be ugly," Mama added. "That's what Christopher Alexander says anyway."

"We have to go to bed," Anders announced, getting up. "Tomorrow is my birthday. I want it to be tomorrow, so we need to go to sleep now."

38. Treasure Hunt

Last week, Anders was eating breakfast with Mama when she had said, "Anders, what would you like to do for birthday? How do you want to celebrate your life?"

"Hmmmm," Anders had said thoughtfully. "I want to wake up and dig. And play with my friends. And do reading with you. And work with Papa!"

"But that's what you do every day," Mama had replied.

"That's what I like to do!" Anders had said.

"How about I make a game for you and your friends to play on your birthday? It's called a treasure hunt," Mama had replied. "There would be clues to follow and at the end a treasure to dig up. Does that sound like fun?"

"Yes!" Anders had said. "But there has to be a lot of digging. Can you bury the treasure very, very, very far down?"

"Of course," Mama had said.

Now it was Anders's birthday. He wrestled with Papa for a long time. Then he read with Mama for a long time. He ate a nice lunch with his family.

Then his friends arrived and at last it was time to do the treasure hunt.

Mama explained the game to the kids: there were ten clues, each clue would lead to another clue, the tenth clue would lead to the treasure. Each clue had one kid's name on it. Only that kid was allowed to read that clue. For that reason, all the kids had to stick together.

The kids were excited. Mama handed a piece of folded up notebook paper to Anders. It had his name written on it—it was his birthday, so he got to go first.

Anders unfolded the paper. It had one word written on it. Anders sounded it out.

"G… a… t… Gate!" Anders shouted.

Because Anders's clue was in English, no one else knew what *gate* meant. But Anders did.

"Mama, it says *gate!*" he said.

"That means that your next clue is hidden… where?" Mama asked him.

"At the gate?" Anders asked.

"Yes," Mama said. "If you go to the gate, you will find your next clue."

"Follow me everyone!" Anders called out in Spanish as he began running down the long driveway to the gate. Yesnir, Jesslyn, Moisés, and Ramón followed him.

At the gate there was another folded-up piece of notebook paper. This one had Yesnir's name written on it, and since Yesnir did not speak English, the clue inside was in Spanish. Yesnir unfolded the paper and read: "*¿Tu quieres nadar?*" Which means: "*Do you want to swim?*

Yesnir, Jesslyn, Moisés, Ramón, and Anders ran as fast as they could to the small swimming pool they liked to play in. Floating in the water inside a plastic bag was another piece of folded-up notebook paper. This one had the name Jesslyn written on it.

Moisés handed the clue to Jesslyn. Jesslyn unfolded it. Jesslyn could not read in any language yet, so her clue was a drawing. It was a drawing of a flowerpot with flowers growing out of it. Jesslyn looked around shyly and pointed to the flowerpot on the patio outside of the bedroom.

The kids ran as fast as they could to the flowerpot. They were so excited that they were talking nonstop, pushing one another in play, laughing and shrieking all the way there. Moisés got to the flowerpot first. He found the next clue. His name was written on it. He read the clue and without even telling anyone else what it said, he began running. The other children ran after him.

The grownups stood around watching. Dolores thought this was the funniest thing she had ever seen. She laughed and laughed. Nate, James, Erick, Mama, and Papa enjoyed it as well. The kids were having a great time.

After running to the big mango tree, where Moisés's clue led, they ran to the chicken coop, the car, the shower, the *jocote* tree, and the fridge. There they got the last clue.

The last clue instructed them to dig in the spot that had been roped off for the new building. Five shovels had been placed at the site of the treasure.

The kids ran all around the roped-off area and found the spot with five shovels. Yesnir and Anders picked up shovels and immediately began digging

The treasure was buried over two feet down. After only a few shovelfuls of dirt, though, Anders stopped digging and, as Jesslyn, Moisés, and Ramón were already doing, just watched Yesnir dig.

"Anders, do you want to do some digging too?" Papa asked.

"No, I'm going to let Yesnir do it," Anders said. "Yesnir is an expert digger. Look how fast he can dig."

It was true. Yesnir dug as well as a grown man.

After five minutes of intense digging in which Yesnir never slowed down or stopped for even a second, he reached a tin box. He pulled it out of the dirt and handed it to Anders. Anders opened it. It had five little bags inside of it, each full of chocolate gold coins.

"Chocolates you guys! Have some!" Anders took a bag for himself and then passed around the tin. Each of the kids took a bag, but they eyed the contents suspiciously. They had never had chocolate before.

To store and sell chocolate required either cool weather or stores with air-conditioning. Their area of Nicaragua had neither weather cool enough to store chocolate without it melting or stores with air conditioning; consequently, the candy sold in their stores was never chocolate. They had had chocolate cookies but never chocolate candy.

Moisés was the first to try a chocolate coin. He liked it. He tried to convince Ramón to try one.

"It's delicious," he said in Spanish. Ramón tried his suspiciously and then smiled. He loved it!

"It is really, really, really good," he told Yesnir.

Yesnir tasted his and agreed. Jesslyn, the most suspicious of all, finally tried hers. She liked it too.

Moisés and Ramón gobbled the rest of their chocolates immediately. Yesnir and Jesslyn each had one more and then put their chocolates aside to bring home to their parents. They loved sharing the strange things to which the Americans introduced them with the rest of their family.

39. Sugar Monster

Anders and his friends played for many hours. Then it was time for his friends to go home. After they left Anders sat down at the table for dinner with Papa, Mama, Nate, and James.

"Mama, I don't want any dinner. I just want cake," Anders said.

"It's your birthday, Anders, so I guess that's okay," Mama said.

Mama looked at Papa. He shrugged. So instead of having dinner, Anders had a big piece of cake. Papa, Mama, Nate, and James ate dinner. Anders helped himself to a second piece of cake. Nate finished his dinner and reached for a piece of cake.

"No!" Anders said. "It's MY cake!"

"Anders this is a pretty big cake," Nate said. "I don't think you can eat the whole thing. Can I have a tiny piece?"

"NO!" Anders said.

"Anders, it's a cake to celebrate your birthday, but it's not your property. It's for everyone," Mama explained.

Now Andes was mad. He got up from the table and stomped his feet. He put two more pieces of cake on his plate. Then suddenly Anders had so much energy in his body that he started running and yelling. He ran around and around in the weeds outside the rancho yelling what sounded like nonsense words that he was making up. Papa and Mama stared at him. Nate and James stared at him.

"What's wrong with him?" Papa asked. "He is not acting like himself at all. I don't even recognize him."

"I think maybe letting Anders have cake for dinner was a bad idea," Mama said. "I had no idea he could act like such a… monster."

"A sugar monster," James said nodding his head knowingly. "This is what kids on sugar act like."

Anders started picking up sticks and small rocks and throwing them as hard as he could at a tree. He was laughing, but it was an aggressive, crazy laugh, not the laugh of a child having a good time.

Then, Anders seemed to get spooked by something. He ran full speed back to the rancho. He didn't stop running when he got there though. He ran straight through the rancho and smacked into the back wall. Then he crumpled onto the floor howling in pain.

Mama ran to him, but he pushed her away. She went to the fridge and got a piece of cheese. She also grabbed a bag of pine nuts.

"Anders," Mama said softly, "you ate too much sugar. You put dessert in your belly and no dinner. Your body wasn't protected from the sugar. I need you to eat this piece of cheese and these pine nuts. Then you will feel better."

"I don't want cheese. I want more cake!" Anders said angrily.

"I can't talk to you about more cake until you eat this cheese," Mama said firmly.

Anders took the cheese and ate it grumpily. Then Mama handed Anders the pine nuts, and he ate them, too. Anders seemed a little calmer and less angry, but he still wasn't himself. He needed time for the sugar to wear off.

Mama got her computer and put on a playlist of home videos for Anders to watch. Soon he was zoned out into the videos.

Papa and Mama breathed a sigh of relief. Nate, James, and Mama helped themselves to pieces of cake. Mama offered Papa a piece, but he declined.

"Seeing what the sugar did to Anders…. It's doing that to us too. We just don't notice it. I don't want it in my body," he said.

"Your self-control has always been one of your most attractive qualities," Mama said.

"I can't believe you let him have cake instead of dinner," James said.

"I guess we just forgot what sugar does to kids since we so rarely eat it," Mama said.

"Having dinner before having dessert is a custom for a reason," Nate said.

"Woe to the man who ignores ancient customs," Mama said.

40. The Straight and Narrow Path

Mama's feet were covered in bug bites. Papa's and Anders's whole bodies were covered in bug bites. They were tired of eating almost nothing but rice, beans, cheese, and soup in a building that only had three sides. They were tired of being harassed by heat, wind, and bugs throughout every meal. They had water now, but life at the farm was still rough. It was time for a break. The family decided to go on an adventure to Rancho Santana.

Rancho Santana was one of the nicest resorts in Nicaragua. Papa and Mama were not wealthy at this point in their lives. They would be one day because wealth is an inevitable consequence of walking the straight and narrow path, but currently their household income put them in the 66th percentile, making them solidly middle class. Because of the offbeat choices they made (like living in Nicaragua half the year where the cost of living was extremely low and preferring to spend money on experiences rather than on things) Papa and Mama had a certain amount of money left over each year with which to have fun.

Rancho Santana was on the west coast of Nicaragua. It took seven hours to drive there from the farm. The last hour was on a dirt road with lots of potholes. By the time they got to the resort, they were exhausted.

Papa parked the car, which was now covered in dust, in a dirt parking lot outside of the main building of the resort. The building was built in an old-world Spanish style, with orange tile floors; white walls; dark wooden doors, window frames, molding, and ceiling beams; colorfully tiled fountains; and iron doorknobs, hinges, curtain rods, and light fixtures.

After they checked in, a bellman in jeans and a polo shirt showed them to their room. Everything was well-made, simple, elegant, and beautiful.

"Anders, what do you think of the style here?" Mama asked.

"I love it!" Anders said. "It's glorious!"

"I agree," Mama said. "When I am in a beautiful place like this, the world feels right. But this style is a little dark and old-fashioned for me. For our farm I want to do something similar, but lighter and with a dash of modernity."

"That sounds great, Mama," Anders said. "Can we go to the pool?"

Everyone was excited to go exploring, so they headed out. From their room, they walked through courtyards and past lawns with fountains until they reached the main social area of the resort. There they found a dining area, with most of the seating outside, and some lawn games. Best of all, there was a large, beautiful pool.

The pool was ovular. It had a shallow end and a deep end like most pools, but unlike most pools, this pool did not have stairs. The shallow end of the pool was only an inch deep at the edge and then had a slope that got deeper and deeper until it reached an island about ten feet in diameter in the center of the pool.

Because the island sat in the middle of the pool, one side of it had quite deep water and the other side had water no deeper than three feet. Anders loved this! He swam to the island in the middle and jumped off. Then he did that again and again.

Soon Papa joined Anders in the pool. Mama got a menu and ordered ceviche, fish tacos, and chips and guacamole. All the food was excellent. Anders liked the ceviche so much that he ate it for almost every meal of their stay at Rancho Santana.

At dinner, when they were eating, Anders noticed some boys at a nearby table looking at him.

"Mama, those boys there are staring at me," he said.

"Oh. Why do you think they are doing that?" Mama asked.

Anders thought for a moment.

"Probably because I'm so cute," he said, perfectly serious. "Because I always keep these dimples on my face."

He smiled to show off his dimples.

"That could be it," Mama said, glancing at the boys Anders was talking about. "Or maybe they want to play with you, but they are shy and don't know how to ask you to play with them."

"Oh," said Anders. "They should come up to me and say, 'Want to play?' And then I will say, 'Yes! I want to play with those balls over there.'"

Anders pointed to the bocce-ball court not far from where they were dining.

"Maybe," Mama said, "since you are not shy, you can help them out by asking if they want to play."

"But I'm eating right now," Anders said.

"Oh, yes," Mama agreed, "you should finish eating first."

When Anders was done eating, he went to the bocce-ball court, picked up a ball, and brought it to the boys who had been staring at him. They understood immediately what he was proposing, and the three boys headed to the bocce-ball court.

Mama turned to the boys' parents and said, "Nice to meet you!"

"Nice to meet you too," they said.

For the rest of the long weekend Anders played with his new friends, swam in the pool, went to the beach, did arts and crafts projects at the Rancho Santana Kids Club, read with Mama, and ate tasty food. He didn't get a single new bug bite during his entire stay, because the resort sprayed for mosquitos every day.

"I don't know about you guys, but this place is making me prefer cancer to bug bites," Papa joked. "You look good, Anders. Your skin has completely healed."

"I'm sad to leave today," Mama said. "I wish we could stay one more day."

"Can we?" Anders asked. "Can we stay many more days? Can we live here?"

"I wish!" Mama said.

"One day, our farm will be as nice as this place, maybe even nicer," Papa said. "But for now, it sure is hard to live there isn't it?"

"So hard," Mama said.

"But you guys, you know we're not going back to the farm right now," Papa reminded them.

"What?!" Anders exclaimed. "I forgot! Where are we going again?"

"We are going to Whistler in Canada. It's December. In the north, they have snow right now. You have never seen snow, Anders. You are going to freak out," he said. "Are you ready to go now that you remember we are headed for the airport and not the farm?"

"Yes, my love," Anders said, immediately heading to the car.

41. Christmas

The Fairmont Chateau in Whistler, British Columbia, was a beautiful hotel that looked like a castle. Now it was decorated for Christmas. There were over a dozen large trees with lights in the arrival courtyard outside the hotel.

The family arrived just after dark. The effect of the Christmas lights was so magical that Anders forgot any tiredness he was feeling from the long day of travel and began running around the minute the car pulled to a stop. It wasn't just the trees that excited him, but also the snow on the ground.

"Look at this!" he called to Mama. "Have you ever been seeing anything so amazing in your whole life?"

"It's breathtaking, Anders," Mama said.

Anders grabbed a handful of snow with his bare hand. Then another handful. He had heard about snow and read about snow, but he had never touched snow before, and he was fascinated by it.

"Why don't I go check in," Papa said with a smile. "I think this may take a while."

"That's a good idea," Mama said.

Mama started rifling through the suitcase she had packed for Anders. In a few seconds she had out his snow coat, mittens, and boots—things she had purchased just for this trip. He gladly put them on and went back to exploring the snow.

"How much longer until you will be ready to go inside and see our hotel room and maybe get some dinner?" Mama asked Anders.

"You know," a good-looking bellman who was standing nearby said to Anders, "there is a lot more snow on the other side of the hotel. It is deep. And there are sleds."

That was all Anders needed to hear. He immediately put down the snow with which he was playing and told Mama he was ready to see the rest of the hotel.

Inside, the hotel was as magical as it was outside. There were Christmas decorations everywhere, including large, fully decorated Christmas trees in every foyer!

Mama and Anders walked through the main lobby, admiring the wreaths, the trees, and the fireplace with the burning fire toward the end.

"This is so lovely," Mama said. "Christmas in Los Angeles has never felt like Christmas to me. *This* feels like Christmas."

"Christmas feels so beautiful," Anders said.

"Yes," Mama agreed.

At the end of the lobby, they reached a cozy dining area, as well decorated as the rest of the hotel.

A variety of delicious smells entered Anders's nose, and suddenly he realized he was hungry.

"Can we have dinner?" Anders asked.

"Yes, please," Mama said. "I'm starving!"

Papa met up with them, and they sat down for a lovey dinner.

Anders ordered a charcuterie plate as he often did. Mama got a delicious seafood soup, and Papa got a steak. Anders made friends with two girls at a nearby table who told him that after dinner they were going swimming. Anders had a difficult decision to make: When dinner was over, did he want to join his new friends at the pool or go sledding?

"The pool is nice," one of the girls told him. "It's very warm. And it has a passageway so you can swim under this curtain thing, and then you are outside. And then it's all cold and snowy, and then you swim back through the passageway and you're inside again, and it's super warm and cozy."

That did it. Anders decided on the pool. He swam with his new friends for several hours. By the time he got out of the pool, he was so tired that he tried to go to sleep on the floor of the elevator on the way to the hotel room.

The next day after having breakfast, Papa, Mama, and Anders got dressed in their snow clothes and headed outside. They borrowed one of the hotel's sleds and joined the horde of other families sledding down the small hill just outside the hotel.

Papa, Mama, and Anders climbed the hill again and again. Sometimes Mama pulled Anders's sled and sometimes Papa did. Anders always pulled it some of the way, but it was too heavy for him to pull it the whole way.

"He could probably get it all the way up if we made him," Papa said.

"Yeah, but where's the fun in that for us?" Mama asked. "Then we just sit at the bottom and watch him sled? I would rather have an excuse to climb this hill again and again. I'm getting so much exercise!"

Anders made several new friends on the sledding hill and invited them all to go swimming with him after dinner.

"Anders, I love how friendly you are," Papa said.

"Me too," Anders agreed. "I have new friends everywhere I go."

"Do you guys know how to make snow angels?" Papa asked Anders and his new friends.

"No," they said.

"What's a snow angel?" Anders asked.

"Okay, watch me," Papa said. "I look around for some nice, smooth snow that hasn't been played in yet, like right here." Papa moved to a spot nearby. "Then, I fall back like this—" Papa fell backward onto his back in the deep snow. "Then I move my arms like this—" Papa's arms were at his sides. He

kept them in the snow and moved them from his sides
to his head, making a circular shape in the snow.
Then he stood up. "Look at the shape I have made,"
Papa said.

"It looks like an angel!" one of the kids said.
"That's why it's called a snow angel," Papa
said.

Now all the kids wanted to make snow angels. They found spots of smooth snow and threw themselves on their backs. Anders loved making snow angels so much that he made at least six before he decided he was done.

"Do you guys want to play hide-and-seek?" he asked the other kids.

They did. Two of the kids ran behind trees nearby. Another buried himself in the snow. Another tried to make a big pile of snow to hide behind. In their brightly colored snow clothes, no one was that hard to find. Hide-and-seek quickly turned into tag. Papa joined Mama on the deck watching the kids.

Several times throughout the morning a man from the hotel came outside and handed out small cups of hot chocolate to all the kids and their parents.

"This is a good moment," Papa said.

"Life doesn't get better than this," Mama agreed.

"This was a tough year. I'm glad we did this," Papa said.

Mama agreed.

The rest of the day was as much fun as the morning had been and the rest of the week was as much fun as their first day was. Anders loved ski school; Papa loved being outside all day every day; and Mama loved that for the first time in many years, it really felt like Christmas.

Afterword

To see what the farm looks like now, go to TheCacaoFarm.com.

If you enjoyed this book, consider checking out my blog, RoslynRoss.blogspot.com. It is private, though, so you will need to email me for an invitation. My email is RoslynRoss@gmail.com.

If you find any errors in this book, please email me and let me know!

Lastly, please consider leaving a review of this book on Amazon.com. I am a self-published author, so every review matters a lot.

Videos

I have created a playlist for this book on my YouTube channel, "Roslyn Ross" (@yesroz). The playlist for this book is called "City Family Farm Family 2." Here is a list of the videos included and a short explanation for them:

Anders Practices Building Skills

Anders helps mix cement for the well.

The Gutted Kitchen

This is a video of the gutted kitchen after the fire.

Anders Eats Sushi (3y)

Anders eats salmon sushi at our favorite sushi restaurant. (He refers to it as *gravlox* in the video.)

Anders Says the Food is Spicy (3y)

> Anders comments on the spiciness of the food at our favorite Indian restaurant.

Anders Jumps on Hay Bales (3y)

> Anders jumps the hay bales at the Renaissance fair.

Anders Climbing (3y)

> Anders climbs safely across the monkey bars.

Anders Cooks Fish (3y)

> Anders cooks some fish for lunch.

Anders Chopping (3y)

> Anders demonstrates safe chopping techniques.

Anders Does Kumon (3y)

> Anders does a Kumon page. He
> practices counting.

Anders Dives (3y)

> Anders spent months jumping into
> the pool and getting right out.

Anders Swims (3y)

> Anders swims in the shallow end of
> a pool at a hotel in Nicaragua.

Anders and the Bucket (3y)

> This is the best video I have of the
> rancho. I do not miss it.

Anders Helps Clear the Spot for the Well (3y)

> Anders helps the guys clear the spot
> for the well-digging truck.

Sounds of the Night

>What the farm sounds like at night
>during the dry season.

Ant Drags Beetle Home for Dinner

>Entertainment at the farm.

The Treasure Hunt

>Anders and his friends do a treasure
>hunt for his birthday.

Papa and Anders Swim at Rancho Santana (4y)

>Papa and Anders swim at Rancho
>Santana.

Anders Pulls his Luggage (4y)

>Anders pulls his own suitcase on our
>way to Whistler.

Liver Fritters Recipe

<u>Ingredients</u>
1 lb. chicken livers
1 cup white flour
Butter
Salt
Pepper

<u>Instructions</u>
1. Carefully go through the chicken livers. Trim off any tendons or parts that appear too tough or too soft. (I only end up keeping about half of the livers.)
2. Cut the remaining liver into half-inch pieces, about the size of a sugar cube.
3. Place the livers in a dish and cover with milk. Place the dish in the fridge for one to three hours or overnight.
4. Put the flour in a shallow bowl.
5. Remove the liver pieces from the milk.
6. Add the liver pieces to the flour and make sure they are nicely coated.
7. Heat a frying pan until hot enough that if you put a few drops of water onto the pan, they instantly turn into little boiling bubbles and bounce around.

That is the perfect temperature. If they don't bounce the pan is too cool. If they instantly turn to steam the pan is too hot.

8. Melt a good amount of butter, enough so that it measures between 1/8 and 1/4 of an inch deep in the pan. (If you have any strained bacon grease, add this to the butter.)

9. Add the coated pieces of liver, making sure they are not touching one another.

10. Cook until browned and crispy on one side, then turn over carefully with a knife and fork.

11. Put a paper towel onto a serving plate.

12. When the liver fritters are nicely browned and crispy on both sides, carefully place them on the paper towel.

13. Salt and pepper to taste.

Anders's Bibliography

Picture Books

Apple Farmer Annie by Monica Wellington

Bathwater's Hot by Shirley Hughes

Cat by Matthew Van Fleet

Charlie the Ranch Dog by Ree Drummond

Dog by Matthew Van Fleet

Flicka, Ricka, Dicka Go to Market by Maj Lindman

Henry and Mudge by Cynthia Ryland

Jet Plane: How It Works by David Macaulay

Moo by Matthew Van Fleet

Our Animal Friends by Alice and Martin Provensen

Pelle's New Suit by Elsa Beskow

Petunia by Roger Duvoisin

Truck Driver Tom by Monica Wellington

Tucker the Tongue Finds His Spot by Joy Moeller

Ultimate Bug-opedia by Darlyne Murawski

What Should Danny Do? by Ganit and Adir Levy

Chapter Books

Where the Red Fern Grows by Wilson Rawls

Five Little Peppers and How They Grew by Margaret
        Sidney

Farmer Boy by Laura Ingalls Wilder

Little House in the Big Woods by Laura Ingalls Wilder

Little House on the Prairie by Laura Ingalls Wilder

On the Banks of Plum Creek by Laura Ingalls Wilder

By the Shores of Silver Lake by Laura Ingalls Wilder

The Long Winter by Laura Ingalls Wilder

Little Town on the Prairie by Laura Ingalls Wilder

These Happy Golden Years by Laura Ingalls Wilder

Workbooks

Whenever a workbook got too hard, we put a bookmark in it and tried it again in three months. Some of these workbooks Anders did not end up finishing until he was four.

Amazing Mazes by Kumon

Brain Quest, age 4-5

Brain Quest, age 5-6

Building Thinking Skills, Beginning 1 by The Critical Thinking Co.

Can You Find Me by The Critical Thinking Co.

Fun Time Phonics by the Critical Thinking Co.

Hooked on Phonics Learn to Read Pre-K

Hooked on Phonics Learn to Read Kindergarten

Logic by Kumon

Mathematical Reasoning by The Critical Thinking Co.

Mind Benders, Level 1 by The Critical Thinking Co.

My Book of Pasting by Kumon

My First Book of Cutting by Kumon
Same and Different by Kumon
Spatial Reasoning by Kumon
Tell Me a Story by The Critical Thinking Co.
Visual Perceptual Skill Building, Book 1 by The
      Critical Thinking Company

Puzzles & Games
100 Board
Cylinder Blocks by Thoth (monochromatic)
Farmyard 2-piece puzzles by Orchard Toys
Guess Who by Hasbro
Jenga by Hasbro
Marble Run Set by Marble Genius
Match It: Head to Tail puzzle by The Learning
      Journey
Montessori Nuts & Bolts by Meroco
Math Wooden Number Shape Set with Learning
      Clock and Lacing Beads by Asher and Olivia
Melissa and Doug 24-piece puzzle
Stomp Rocket
Wooden Sorting & Stacking Toy by Pebira
Wooden Jigsaw Puzzles by Melissa and Doug

Apps
Audubon Guides
Montessori 100 Board
Montessori Counting Board by GrashopperAps
Montessori Numbers by L'Escapadou

Montessori Writing Wizard by L'Escapadou

<u>Classes</u>
Gymnastics
Kumon
Piano

<u>Field Trips in the Los Angeles Area</u>
California Science Center
Petersen Automotive Museum
Getty Art Museum
Getty Villa Museum
Griffith Observatory
Huntington Library, Art Museum, and Botanical
   Gardens
KidSpace Children's Museum
Natural History Museum of Los Angeles County
Renaissance fair

<u>YouTube</u>
WranglerStar

<u>Television and Movies</u>
We do not own a television, so any shows or movies
are watched on a computer.

At this age Anders watched three types of things:
construction shows, documentaries on any animals he
was interested in, and documentaries on what it is like

to survive without modern civilization. I consider these the three educational areas of: practical life, preparation for science, and preparation for history.

Television
Building Hawaii on HGTV
House Hunters: Off the Grid on HGTV
Hotel Amazon on the Travel Channel
Insane Pools on Animal Planet
Animal documentaries on Nature, PBS, BBC
Live Free or Die on National Geographic
Man, Woman, Wild on Discovery

Movies
A Cow's Life
An Original Duckumentary
Babies
Little Hard Hats: Farm Country Ahead
Little Hard Hats: Fire and Rescue
Little Hard Hats: House Construction Ahead
Little Hard Hats: Road Construction Ahead
Little Hard Hats: Where the Garbage Goes
March of the Penguins
More than Honey
Oceans by DisneyNature
The Crimson Wing by DisneyNature

Acknowledgments

Tom — Thank you for your support.

Anders and Henrik — Thank you for your feedback and ideas.

Nate and James — Thank you for the memories we share and for being part of this adventure.

Ken and Carmen — Thank you for the truly endless support and for the sugar-on-Sundays idea.

Erick Gonzalez — Thank you for all the good advice you have given us over the years.

Kathi Ratner – Thank you for being my friend and for being there when I needed you.

Cynthia Keller-Bennett — Thank you for the work-party idea.

Alexander Cohen — Thank you for your editing services.

Made in United States
Troutdale, OR
07/26/2024

21545482R00137